NO AND YES

On the Genesis of Human Communication

NO AND YES

On the Genesis of Human Communication

RENÉ A. SPITZ, M.D.

International Universities Press, Inc.

NEW YORK   NEW YORK

TO MY WIFE

Contents

Foreword

THIS IS the sixth in a series of investigations on the onto-genetic beginnings of man, on the processes through which the species achieves the dignity of the human being. Its sub-ject is the inception of semantic and verbal communication, the beginning of thought processes and concept formation. The previous studies treated of the ontogenesis of percep-tion ("The Primal Cavity"), of the ontogenesis of social rela-tions ("The Smiling Response"), of the development of object relations ("The Genesis of the First Object Rela-tions"*), of the earliest stages of sexuality ("Autoerotism"), and of the development and differentiation of drives and affects ("Anxiety in Infancy" and "Aggression: Its Role in the Establishment of Object Relations").

With the present study we are carrying our investigations one step further in the life of the infant, into his second year. Our eventual aim is to combine these successive ex-plorations and those we plan to make in the future into an over-all picture, in which the ontogenesis of the ego, the un-folding and formation of object relations, the foundation and the establishment of personality structure, and the ultimate achievement of social relations will be presented from a psy-choanalytic viewpoint. The opportunity to continue this re-

* An English edition of this work is now in preparation and is expected to appear in 1958.—Editor's note.

search has been afforded the author through the generous hospitality of Dr. Herbert Gaskill. As Head of the Department of Psychiatry of the Medical Center of the University of Colorado, he has made available the resources of his department most liberally for our further research.

The point of departure of the present inquiry may seem trivial and hardly important when considered in the light of the fundamental problems of psychosis and neurosis, with which psychoanalysis is usually concerned. Neither does it seem important when we think in terms of the problems of the organization, of the structure and of the function of the human psyche. But these are problems, I think, which in their major part have been answered or at least outlined by Freud. However, a number of details remain to be explored within these outlines. Our present purpose will be to apply to such details the tools with which Freud provided us.

Accordingly, in our investigations we examined minutely one or the other of the building blocks on which Freud's ideas rest; at the same time we have endeavored to keep in sight the place and the function of each of these blocks within the idea as a whole.

It is in this sense that we offer the present study. It is in this sense that we believe the minute examination of earliest infantile behavior to be justified. It is finally in this sense that our extensive attempts to place our propositions within the theoretical framework of the metapsychological viewpoint on the one hand, of the structural viewpoint on the other, have been undertaken.

I wish to acknowledge my indebtedness to Dr. Bertram D. Lewin, whose penetrating discussion of some of my ideas prompted me to examine them more thoroughly. In the course of this process, what originally was a rather brief article on one or two findings grew into the present monograph. The questions he raised stimulated me to seek answers in a number of disciplines such as embryology, neurophysiology, animal ethology, infant pathology, etc. Each of these provided answers which could be synthesized with my own findings and moreover proved pregnant with new ideas. The final result of this synthesis is the present monograph.

I also wish to thank Drs. George Engel and Franz Reichsman of Rochester for their generous permission to observe the case of Monica and to use my observations as well as their material.

I am greatly indebted to Mr. Geoffrey Cobliner for his unfailing devotion in helping me to find and put together the bibliographic sources used in the present study, as well as for his critical assistance in the sharper and more precise formulation of the concepts, definitions and propositions elaborated here.

Special thanks go to Miss Lottie M. Maury, Editor of International Universities Press, for pointing out omissions in the sequence of ideas presented, for her suggestions regarding the balance and sequence of the manuscript and for her selfless help in working through the whole manuscript with me from these viewpoints. But in addition she contributed essentially to the value of this study by preparing the Index, a task which only someone with her scholarly knowledge of psychoanalytic literature could have performed with such competence.

I cannot end the list of my acknowledgements without once again returning to Freud. Not only are the ideas on which this monograph is based inspired by his work, the motivation to undertake this task itself can be found in the remark contained in his article on "The Antithetical Sense of Primal Words":

[xi]

"We shall understand the language of the dream better and translate it easier, if we know more about the development of language."

In concluding I may be permitted to mention a more personal motivation: This study originated as the draft of a brief paper to be presented on the occasion of the celebration of the Freud Centenary. It was planned to explore how Freud's ideas on Negation, expressed thirty years ago, could be applied to direct infant observation. But the inherent logic of ideas carried my exploration far beyond its modest beginning. Nevertheless, the intention remains: The author still considers it his contribution to the Freud Centenary, even if belated.

Denver, 1957   R.A.S.

NO AND YES

On the Genesis of Human Communication

NO AND YES

*In analysis we never discover
a "No" in the unconscious. . . .*

—FREUD (1925)

1.

Introduction

PSYCHOANALYSIS as a method of investigation uses as its tool communication, both verbal and nonverbal. This fact is such a commonplace that it is hardly ever mentioned explicitly. It is surprising how little has been published by psychoanalysts on communication[1] and how isolated from each other the handful of books and articles on the subject have been (Kris, Speier, et al., 1944; Kasanin, 1944; Rapaport, 1951; Meerloo, 1952; Mittelmann, 1954; Loewenstein, 1956). The scattered statements in the literature are mostly concerned with verbal communication. There is even less on nonverbal communication. Felix Deutsch (1947, 1949, 1952) was the first to publish an extensive study on the meaning of postural changes during analytic treatment.

As for the ontogenesis of verbal and nonverbal communication, the only articles on this problem which have come to my attention are those of Hug-Hellmuth (1919, 1921), Spielrein (1922), Kulovesi (1939), Sugar (1941), Christoffel (1950), Greenson (1954).

The earliest mention of the subject is made by Hug-Hellmuth. Her statements, in even greater measure than those of

---

1 We will call communication any perceivable change of behavior, be it intentional or not, directed or not, with the help of which one or several persons can influence the perception, the feelings, the emotions, the thoughts or the actions of one or several persons, be that influence intended or not.

Spielrein, consist of adultomorph attributions of meanings to infantile oral behavior; they are either not supported by observation, or are sweeping generalizations from a single observed case to all infants. Kulovesi's statements in a brief paper are equally unconvincing and do not contribute much to our understanding of the subject.

In contrast with these, Christoffel's article on fetal and early infantile behavior, though not based on personal observations, is replete with observational data and reports culled from the contemporary and older literature. It is to be regretted that it was not followed up and more fully developed.

It is obvious that psychoanalysts, who deal mainly with the verbal communications of the adult, will have to undertake a more systematic study of the earliest, archaic forms of communication in infancy if they want to arrive at an understanding of adult communication on one hand, and the beginnings of thought process on the other. In view of the fact that the genetic aspects of psychoanalysis are stressed so consistently, it is surprising that such a study has not been undertaken long ago.

It is all the more surprising because we find that Freud not only saw this clearly from the beginning, but also said so quite explicitly. It would be gratuitous to pursue the many forms in which he described the connections between verbal function and thought processes. As for nonverbal manifestations, it is worth while to go back to Freud's illuminating and earliest formulation in the "Project for a Scientific Psychology" (1895a). There, speaking of an effort to discharge an impetus released along motor pathways, he states that the first path to be followed is that leading to internal change (e.g., emotional expression, screaming or vascular innervation). He further says that this discharge in itself could not result in relief of tension. Tension relief can only be achieved by action leading to alteration in the external world; this action the human organism is incapable of achieving in its early stages. Therefore, extraneous help has to be enlisted to relieve the child's condition, e.g., with the help of screaming. And he states: "This path of discharge thus acquires an extremely important secondary function—viz. of bringing about an understanding[2] with other people; and the original helplessness of human beings is thus the primal source of all moral motives."

This momentous statement was written in 1895. It contains all the fundamentally necessary insights into the roots of communication. It clearly assigns two functions to this earliest process: from the subjective point of view of the newborn, this "communication" is only a discharge process. However, this discharge process which from the infant's point of view is an expression of his internal state is perceived by the mother as an appeal for her help. She will react to it and relieve the infant's tension (for instance, feed him when he is hungry). Thus the undirected discharge process of the infant achieves a result through extraneous help. This cycle which will be consistently repeated thus constitutes the beginning of communication and of object relation.

The infant's attempt at direct motor discharge of tension is in itself unsuccessful, but as its by-product a secondary function of the selfsame process is developed. Freud discusses this in a later chapter of the same monograph.

The establishment of this secondary function of discharge, namely, the infant's directed communication, belongs to a more advanced stage of development. Its prerequisite is that perception and memory be already developed in the infant,

[2] In the original German Freud (1895) used the term *Verständigung*, which in this context refers primarily to communication.

so that he can link the auditive perception of his own discharge screaming with the memory trace of the tension relief
offered thereupon by the environment. Though already an
advanced cycle in the infant's mental development, this is
still a very early precursor of verbal communication. The
infant's communication operates on this archaic level for
many months before verbal communication originates
from it.

What we intend to investigate in our present study is preverbal communication. That is, we will investigate phenomena occurring a long time before the use of words, let alone
language proper is acquired.

It will serve to clarify our concepts if we try to enumerate
the successive steps in the process of acquiring verbal communication. The first of these steps is the direct discharge of
tension in the neonate. This is the step which I have discussed
in the article "The Primal Cavity" (1955a). In the next step
of the infant's development a secondary function of this
discharge process is acquired; the infant, having developed
the functions of perception and memory, links his own discharge screaming with the tension relief offered by the environment. In the terms of Karl Buehler's (1934) language
theory, in which he distinguishes within the total phenomenon of language three functions, namely expression, appeal,
and description, the first step just described is expression,
while the second step is appeal. Buehler intentionally limited his approach to the descriptive function of language.

Our focus of interest will be a phenomenon which cannot
be classified in the terms of Buehler's three categories. Nevertheless, chronologically it coincides with the unfolding and
acquisition of the second step. This phenomenon is the beginning of intentional communication.

But even this statement must be qualified. The term

[6]

"communication" is usually misunderstood and assumed to apply only to volitionally directed, reciprocal exchange of signals. However, the signs of processes taking place in beings, who have no intention of communicating anything whatsoever, are also a form of communication. An example for this can be found in the instrument on which communication was studied earliest, namely in the telephone. When the telephone rings, an intentional signal addressed to us is being produced, informing us that a communication is to be expected through the telephone at this moment. But when we are near our telephone, and we happen to hear a low buzzing sound, then we realize that the receiver is off the hook. What we are hearing is the dial tone which we use as an indicator informing us of the state of the telephone; but it is not an intentional communication directed at us. The kind of communication which we will examine in the infant is of the same nature as the dial tone of the telephone—at least that part of it which will serve as the jumping-off point of this investigation. This communication is manifested through certain changes in the general behavior of the infant, mostly of a transitory nature. These changes are not performed for the purpose of informing us of anything; but they do tell us something about what goes on in the infant. They are self-centered like the language of animals. Bierens de Haan (1929) introduced an excellent formulation to distinguish animal language from human language when he defined animal language as egocentric[3] and human language as allocentric. The communications we are investigating in the infant are egocentric, for they are discharge phenomena,

3 De Haan's use of the term egocentric is unrelated to the psychoanalytic meaning of the concept "ego." Egocentric for de Haan means "centered in the subject." By calling animal language egocentric, de Haan conveys that it is not addressed to another individual, but is the expression of inner processes. The same is the case for the neonate in whom the ego does not exist.

undirected and unintentional, in response to inner processes. Even when such discharge occurs as a result of external stimulation, it is not a response to the stimulus itself. Rather it is the result of processes provoked in the infant by the stimulus. Thus, even when the neonate responds to the stimulus, the response is only an indicator of processes going on in his interior.

I wish to stress that it is only in the sense of an indicator that the neonate's behavior can be considered as a communication; but since the neonate's behavior does communicate something to us, we can use this behavior as the starting point of our investigation.

It should not be forgotten, however, that communications in the nature of indicators do not occur only in the normal, healthy infant, but also in pathological cases. Indeed, in these cases we are apt to pay particular attention to such communications; it is in such conditions that the indicator is recognized by everyone as a symptom of what is going on in the infant. Thus communications occurring in pathological processes alert us to the fact that all manifestations at this early age are indicators of processes both pathological and normal going on within the subject. As in so many other instances in psychoanalytic research, we can conclude here from pathology to that which obtains for the normal. We will therefore include in our approach also the careful investigation of infant manifestations in pathological conditions.

2.

A Behavior Pattern Peculiar to Deprived Children

Among the observations which I made on babies suffering from the hospitalism syndrome (Spitz, 1945a), there is one particular behavior which was manifested after these children had been deprived of emotional supplies for prolonged periods. Breast fed on the average during the first three months of life, the ninety-one children in question had then been separated from their mothers for periods of six months to a year. Accordingly they ranged in age from nine months to one year and a half. On my approach or on that of anybody else (excepting the nurses who approached them with food at the time of feeding) a number of these infants would rotate their heads around the sagittal axis of the spinal column. This behavior, which closely resembled the universally familiar head-shaking pattern of the grownup in whom it signifies "No," continued as long as a stranger confronted them.

When alone and undisturbed, these children were quiet enough. They would lie supine; when they became active, their main activity consisted in bizarre finger movements. They would watch the movements of their fingers for prolonged periods, sometimes for hours. Head-rolling, somewhat in the nature of spasmus nutans, was present in one

[9]

isolated instance. Head-banging was not observed. They might clutch their garments, and, as in forced grasping, be unable to relinquish their grip, dragging the garment into the weirdly waving pattern of their hand activity. When particularly active, they would also lift their legs and clutch at their socks and toes. These few activities encompass all that these children suffering from hospitalism did. These activities occurred only, if at all, in the early stages of deprivation. Autoerotic activities, including thumb-sucking, were practically nonexistent. In the more advanced stages these children would sink into lethargy, lying without movement or sound, staring into space as if in a daze. The approach of anyone, outside that of the nurses at the hour of feeding, evoked manifest unpleasure.

It was quite evident that these children resented the disturbance introduced by the approach of any human being. It was equally evident that such an approach, that the attempt to make contact with them, required them to abandon their lethargy and to use energy, of which they had little, in responding to the perception and approach of any person. The more advanced the deprivation, the more enfeebled the waning energies were and the more immediate the refusal of contact. This refusal had one consistent element: the rotation of the head around the sagittal axis. In the earlier stages this might be accompanied by screaming, particularly if the observer did not withdraw. In the later stages the crying would turn into a thin wailing and begin immediately on approach, accompanied by rotation of the head; in the most advanced stages the wailing would be only a whimper.

The vocalization accompanying this activity had at all stages an unpleasure quality. From here on we will speak of this head-rotating behavior with a term borrowed from Tilney

[10]

and Casamajor (1924) as "cephalogyric motions." In view of the unpleasure quality of the vocalization connected with these motions, we will qualify them as "negative cephalogyric motions," because from the psychological viewpoint of the observer they signify unpleasure in the infant.

3.

Negative Cephalogyric Motions

NEGATIVE cephalogyric motions are basically different from what is commonly called head-rolling, with which all infant observers are familiar. The difference consists in that head-rolling occurs spontaneously regardless of the presence or absence of another person, and not in response to an environmental stimulus. It belongs to the category of pathological behavior classified as spasmus nutans.

Spasmus nutans was first described in 1850 by Faber; the literature contains many and mostly unsatisfactory explanations of the phenomenon which we can disregard for our purposes. The more recent discussions by Raudnitz (1897), Zappert (1924), Finkelstein (1938), and others, concur in describing an activity that is more or less independent of environmental stimuli. Indeed, many authors attribute it to the infants' living in dark rooms *without stimulation*. It has come to be more and more considered as originating from some inner reason; in other words, the various authors consider it a spontaneous activity of the infant.

In this it is in sharp contrast to negative cephalogyric motions, which bear the unmistakable character of an interpersonal response. Negative cephalogyric motions do not occur when the infant is alone, but only when he is approached by somebody. It is not a swinging of the head set up by neural reflexes, it is not a pure discharge movement like head-rolling and head-banging.

Negative cephalogyric motions are also quite distinct from the manifestations signifying refusal of contact shown by healthy, normal children when confronted with strangers in the second half of the first and the beginning of the second year. These healthy children do not rotate their heads; they cover their eyes, they lower their heads or turn them away, they hide their faces behind their skirts or in the blankets. They may manifest rocking behavior. But we have never observed them signifying refusal of contact by rotating their heads as an adult would to signify negation.

If negative cephalogyric motions are not a neural reflex, nor used by the normal child in similar circumstances as the deprived children and at a comparable age, they might still be a learned social signal. At the age level of eight months to a year, head-shaking as a sign of negation and as a social signal has not been described in the normal child; nor have I seen it in the course of my own observations. On the average, the normal child learns to *understand* the adult's negating or prohibiting headshake in the first trimester of the second year. We see, of course, many advanced children who *understand* this signal already before the completion of the first year, somewhere between the tenth and twelfth month. But as an intentional signal, this gesture is used only by children later in the second year of life.

In the case of the emotionally deprived children observed by us, the use of a social gesture before the end of the first year appears even more highly improbable than in the normal child, for they had no opportunity to learn it; they were offered a small fraction, if any, of the number and variety of social signals offered to children raised under normal circumstances and in families. There were so few nurses that the nursing personnel barely had the time to "prop" the bottle with the nipple in the child's mouth, and after that to diaper the child at stated hours. There was no question of their offering the child any social signal, be that in the nature of prohibition or in that of permission. Nor were they motivated to do it, for the nursing personnel was not encouraged to educate these children.

In view of these considerations, we offer the hypothesis that negative cephalogyric motions might be a meaningful behavior in terms of the particular personality which develops in the emotionally deprived infant; but we must further assume that since the child has not learned this meaning from the environment through imitation, this behavior is probably connected to a pattern which was present at an earlier developmental stage. Consequently we must proceed to investigate whether this is not a preformed behavior pattern, and whether the situation in which it originally appeared might not have been quite different from the one in which we observed the behavior in deprived children.

4.

The Ontogenesis of Cephalogyric Behavior

In the past the origin and the vicissitudes of behavior patterns have attracted primarily the attention of psychologists. In more recent years they have become the subject matter of a new discipline, that of animal ethology. Among psychologists, Karl Buehler's (1924) formulation on the organization of behavior is perhaps the most concise and convincing.[1] He states that behavior is progressively segregated out of the random disorganized movements of the newborn through the conservation of success-specific movements[2] on one hand, and the simultaneous elimination of unsuccessful movements on the other. The goal-specific movements will then be organized into a goal-directed pattern.[3]

This proposition was explored by McGraw (1935), who investigated infant behavior patterns, their origin, their development and their modifiability. She distinguished phylogenetically preformed patterns from ontogenetically acquired

[1] Buehler elaborated an idea also expressed by Taine (1876): "In my opinion it is out of the enormous number of movements, constantly essayed, that there will be evolved by gradual selection, the intentional movements having an object and attaining it."

[2] Success-specific in terms of need gratification, intention and goal.

[3] Similar concepts have been developed recently by Sylvia Brody in her book *Patterns of Mothering* (1956).

[15]

ones. The phylogenetically preformed patterns have to be abandoned in the course of development, because they occur in a reflex-like compulsive fashion and therefore will subsequently interfere with intentional action. An example of this is the grasping function. In grasping the original clutch reflex is brought under control of volition through the capacity of innervating intentionally the antagonists of the flexors, an achievement which is acquired toward the sixth month. From here on grasping becomes more and more an aim-directed activity endowed with meaning (Spitz, 1951).

In the course of this development a behavior pattern which had begun as a reflex action is brought under the control of the mind. What was first purely neural and muscular, has now an added dimension, a psychological function (Sherrington, 1906). This function can be lost again in frontal lobe lesions, where we see forced grasping reappear. However, as soon as the neural and muscular movements are brought under the control of the mind, they will be used in a purposive manner for achieving an aim. It is this purpose which transforms the movement into a behavior and into an action directed by the psyche.

Just like aim-directed grasping, negative cephalogyric motion in the emotionally deprived children is a volitional movement. The percept which provokes it is the approaching person's attempt to make contact with the child. We may assume that the meaning of negative cephalogyric motion is a refusal of contact, as evinced by the vocalization which accompanies it and by the concomitant expression of unpleasure.

We must not, however, let ourselves be misled through the phenotypical similarity of the deprived infant's cephalogyric motions with the head-shaking "No" gesture used by ourselves. True, these children are refusing, just as we refuse when we shake our head. But we cannot, as we have shown previously, assign any understanding of these semantic signals to these children. They are using a movement which, as a neuromuscular pattern, is available to the infant from the beginning. But, as we have mentioned on page 13, such movements are put into the service of directed intentional communication in children twice as old at the earliest. In the first year of life other preformed patterns to express refusal of contact are more readily available to the child.

Avoidance

The most plausible preformed behavior pattern under the circumstances would be the avoidance reaction. Watson (1924) situates this reaction, which he calls flight, at the very beginning of life. He postulates that this is one of the three basic behavior patterns observable in the neonate.[4] What he calls the flight reaction can certainly be observed in the form of avoidance movements, and turning away from unpleasure (though at a considerably later age than stated by Watson) in the latter part of the first six weeks.

However, a careful observation of the negative cephalogyric motions shows convincingly that this is no avoidance behavior. For the purposes of avoiding the stimulation by the approaching adult, turning the head to the side and not looking back at him would be far more economical and effective measures.[5] But far from turning their heads aside and diverting their glance, these deprived infants look straight at the

4 We will not go into the question whether Watson's assumptions are borne out by the facts and whether all three behavior patterns posited by him, namely flight, fight, and love, can really be observed in the neonate or not.

5 That this conclusion is correct was confirmed when, thanks to the courtesy of Drs. Engel and Reichsman, I had the opportunity to observe and to make some experiments on an infant with congenital atresia esophagi and gastric fistula. In what follows we will present some further observations made on this case.

[17]

approaching person and do not take their eyes off them. We may therefore assume that avoidance behavior is not the preformed pattern for negative cephalogyric motion.

Avoidance behavior, however, cannot be conceived only in terms of directed, purposive *physical* behavior in the nature of flight or of turning away; as psychoanalysts we are familiar with the use of psychological devices for the purpose of avoidance; phobia, for instance, can take the place of flight and scotomization or denial that of turning away.

One such method of psychological avoidance which we find both in adults and children is regression. Particularly children and infants, when confronted with unpleasure, may resort to regressive behavior patterns which have nothing to do with the manifestly unpleasure-provoking stimulus. The behavior resorted to does not remove the stimulus or weaken it; it need not be meaningful in terms of the objective environmental factors of which the unpleasure situation consists. But it is meaningful in providing a discharge of tension or at least a reduction in the increase of the tension produced by the external situation.

The thumb-sucking of frustrated children is a good example of such regressive behavior. It does not do anything to remove the frustration with which the child finds itself confronted. It provides a reduction of the tension created through the frustration by enabling the child to regress to that stage at which all frustration, as well as all gratification, is of an oral nature. Through this regression the thumb-sucking child makes an attempt to achieve autonomy from the unpleasurable environment, possibly with concomitant hallucinatory gratifications. This proposition becomes even more plausible if we consider the frequency with which thumb-sucking leads to sleep and, we may assume, to dreaming.

In view of the fact that negative cephalogyric motion is

[18]

not related to spasmus nutans, not comparable to refusal of contact by normal infants, not a learned social signal, nor a purposive avoidance, I asked myself whether it could not be a regressive behavior like thumb-sucking. Accordingly, I examined the neonatal behavior pattern for a possible prototype for negative cephalogyric motion. I believe I found one such prototype in the "rooting" behavior of the newborn, who, when put to nurse at the breast, seeks the nipple with quite similar cephalogyric motions of the head. Moreover, investigation of the literature shows that this behavior is to be found not only in the human infant but also has a considerable phylogenetic background, for it has been extensively observed and described in mammals.

Rooting Behavior

Rooting behavior has attracted the attention of experimental psychologists, pediatricians, neurologists, and, more recently, animal ethologists and psychoanalysts. Experimental psychological descriptions, which begin already with S. Pepys' diary (1667), and to name only a few of the successors, Darwin (1873), Kussmaul (1859), Preyer (1893), Bernfeld (1925), Rippin and Hetzer (1930), Gesell (1954), Pratt (1946) and many others, mention various aspects of the phenomenon, but do not give anywhere near the total range of its details.

I was able to capture its major features in my investigations of earliest neonatal behavior through a series of motion pictures of a total of twenty-four neonates delivered without anesthetics, immediately after birth and during their first breast-feeding.[6] These motion pictures show that touching

[6] A film made recently by the Max-Planck Institute für Verhaltensforschung under the direction of Konrad Lorenz by Prechtl and Sylvia Klimpfinger has come to my attention which shows this behavior both in mammal and human in beautiful detail. We will refer to this film, *Entwicklung der frühkindlichen Motorik* (Prechtl, 1955), in discussing the details of the motor pattern below.

[19]

the perioral region (the "snout" for short) of the baby acts as
a stimulus which triggers the rooting behavior. If we touch
the perioral region with our finger, the infant turns his head
toward this stimulus and performs a snapping motion of the
mouth. When, however, the stimulus consists in the maternal
breast touching his face, the infant will rotate his head from
right to left and back again in a number of rapid sweeps,
his mouth half open, until the mouth encounters the nipple
and the lips close around it. At this point the rotation of
the head is stopped and sucking begins.

The behavior pattern of rooting is manifestly congenital,
for, as my motion pictures show, it can be elicited immediately after birth in the first minutes of neonatal life. From
the reflexological point of view I am inclined to make the
following assumption: The reflex consists in turning the head
toward the stimulus. If the breast is this stimulus and touches
the left cheek of the infant, a rotation to the left occurs until
the right cheek comes in contact with the breast. At this
point the head is turned back again toward the right from
which the new stimulus comes. These alternate stimulations
of the "snout" evoke the behavior. The open mouth makes it
possible for the nipple to be lodged in the mouth during
these sweeps of the head.

Rangell (1954), probably basing himself on much earlier
neurological publications, spoke of this as an orientation
behavior. Neurologists have shown this behavior to be an
inborn and not a learned one. It is not only present at birth
but, as shown by Minkowski (1922), is already demonstrable
in fetuses beginning with three months of age. Minkowski's
observations on fetal behavior were continued by Davenport
Hooker (1939, 1952), with a most exact technique and recorded in impressive motion pictures. It is of particular
interest that the first reflexogenic area is restricted to the

[20]

nose-mouth region in the beginning, but from the beginning includes movements of the body, among them the Magnus -de Kleyn (1912, 1924) postural reflexes. A few weeks after the first appearance of oral reactions to the stimulation of the snout the fetus will also react to palmar stimulation by closing his fingers. The early appearance in fetal life of mouth and hand reactions is noteworthy in view of the co-ordination of these two behavior patterns in the first month of life during sucking activity. To the psychoanalyst, this mouth-hand coordination is familiar from the work of Isakower (1938) and of Hoffer (1949, 1950). I have discussed its role extensively in a previous publication (1955a). Min-kowski's findings raised the question at what level of cerebral integration the elementary survival behavior of nursing becomes available and what the factors involved in this behavior are. Gamper (1926), in a most informative study on a mesencephalic monster, provided much information on this question. In his careful survey of the literature Gamper established that sucking and swallowing behavior is observable in anencephalic monsters which did not have any brain development above the level of the medulla oblongata. The case observed by Gamper was carefully recorded in motion pictures and protocols, and eventually a complete cytologic workup of the brain was made.

He clearly distinguishes two stages in the rooting behavior, the first of which he calls an *oral orientation reflex,* whereas the second is the *prehension of the stimulus* by the lips. A brief synopsis of some of his findings in his own terms shows that asymmetric (unilateral) stimulation of the perioral region triggers the oral orientation reflex (*oraler Einstellautomatismus*). This consists in the opening of the mouth and in an adversive rotation of the head in the direction of the stim-ulus, together with a snapping movement. The condition governing the functioning of the trigger stimulus is that the stimulation be unilateral or, as Gamper puts it, asymmetrical. In other words, the stimulus may only touch circumscribed areas located laterally on the upper or on the lower lip. As soon as the stimulation becomes symmetrically centered, that is touching *simultaneously* upper *and* lower lip, the orientating rotation ceases, the lips clamp down on the stimulus and sucking movements begin.

I wish to stress in this description the element of the *simultaneous* stimulation of upper and lower lip. I believe that the simultaneous stimulation of upper and lower lip represents two *discrete* stimuli which are linked, in an additive process, to what has been called in animal ethology *Reizsummations-Phaenomen*—in Tinbergen's words, "the law of heterogeneous summation" (1951). It is further noteworthy that Gamper calls this process "oral grasping" and equates it with the grasping and forced grasping of the hand. Both oral and hand grasping are subcortically localized and both are to be found in anencephalic newborns up to the level of the medulla oblongata.

The finding that the rooting behavior is innate and operates already on mesencephalic level prompts us to seek analogous behavior in the nonhuman mammals and perhaps even in nonmammals. The literature of animal ethology provides us with several well-documented studies of such behavior. In mammals it has been described in the feeding behavior of calves, of cats, of dogs, hares, rabbits, guinea pigs and hamsters, and brought into relation with equally careful observations of the nursing behavior of the human infant.

5.

A Digression into Phylogenesis

To begin with, it should be noted that infrahuman animals fall into two major classes with fundamentally different feeding behavior. These classes are the altricial (*Nesthocker*) and the precocial (*Nestflüchter*).[1] From the definition of these two classes it appears that man, born helpless and requiring nursing, help and care for a long time, relatively immature at birth (Bolk, 1926), belongs behaviorally to the class of the altricials.[2]

Analogies drawn between the behavior of man and that of animals which belong to the class of the precocials (as, for instance, the chicken in the case of birds, and the calf or sheep in the case of mammals) have to be considered with the greatest skepticism. Our caution will go even beyond

[1] *Altricial* (from the Latin *altrix*, nurse) is the zoological term for the species whose young are born in an immature and helpless condition so as to require care and nursing for some time after the birth; *precocial* (from the Latin *praecox*, premature) designates animals whose young at birth are covered with down and are able to run about.

[2] This statement has to be qualified by mentioning at least one of the proponents of a different opinion. Adolf Portmann (1951, 1956) considers man a precocial who has deviated into altricial patterns. Indeed, he calls man a full-fledged evolutionary form in its own right and considers culture our "second nature." This concept is not far removed from Hartmann's proposition that man is equipped with a specialized organ of adaptation, i.e., with the ego. It is mainly to this independent organization that adjustment is entrusted in man, while instincts mediate adjustment in animals (Hartmann, 1939; also Hartmann, Kris, Loewenstein, 1946).

[23]

that used in comparing beings which differ from each other only in the level of their psychological integration. Within certain limits it is more permissible to compare human behavior and rat behavior, for both are altricials, than to compare man, an altricial, with the chicken or the calf, a precocial (Spitz, 1955).

This last statement, however, is not to be construed as a justification to explain human psychological processes with the help of the behavior of other altricials.

The study of behavior in nonhuman animals can provide us only with the embryology of behavior. That is an approach introduced by Konrad Lorenz (1950), who was able with its help to establish the relatedness of morphologically seemingly quite different species and the unrelatedness of morphologically seemingly similar ones. Viewed in this fashion, man appears far closer to the altricials than to the precocials, as will be seen further on.

This distinction is not an egregious one. It is self-evident that in the adaptation of the precocial, environment plays a basically different role from the one it plays in the adaptation of the altricial. The precocial animal has to have at its disposal a vast range of innate inherited behavior patterns to ensure its survival as an individual (and also as a species). Consequently, learning and the influence or the changes of the environment will play a relatively small role in the adaptation of the precocial individual to its surroundings. Adaptation in the precocial is not a matter of ontogeny, it is a matter of phylogeny; it is not the individual which adapts, the adaptive changes take place in the species as a result of phylogenetic modifications. That entails the sacrifice of hecatombs of lives.

Matters are quite different in the altricial. During the period of helplessness, survival behavior can be acquired

[24]

through learning from the maternal nourisher and protector. Therefore, only relatively few innate behavior patterns are necessary to ensure the altricials' survival. The protected nursing period and helplessness make the transmittal of individual experience possible *during* ontogenesis. Even radical environmental changes during the individual's life need not make survival impossible. Adaptive processes during ontogenesis ensure autoplastic modifications, performed by the individual himself, with the help of which he adjusts to such changes. This is different in principle from the above mentioned rigidity of inborn behavior patterns in the precocials. These rigid patterns form an obstacle and practically preclude adaptation during ontogenesis. Therefore, in the precocial, adaptation can only take place through the survival of the fit and the annihilation of astronomical numbers of the unfit. The ontogenetic adaptation of the altricial, in contrast to this, is spectacularly parsimonious. One is inclined to postulate the principle of parsimony in material and energy expended as one of the guiding principles of evolution. This is particularly impressive when we compare the mechanism underlying behavior in paramecium, as opposed to that in man.

In paramecium, behavior is based on action governed by the trial-and-error principle. In man, behavior is based on a thought process. The scanning process of human thought is also a trial-and-error procedure. But instead of the huge quanta of muscular energy required for action, the thought process takes place with the help of the displacement of minimal quanta of energy in an *experimental* action along memory traces (Freud, 1911).

Thought processes and a capacity for reasoning are acquired during "learning," which consists in autoplastic modifications during the ontogenesis of the individual on one

[25]

hand, through the transmission of parental experience in the course of nurture, on the other. In terms of psychoanalytic theory, we would say that it takes place through the instrumentality of object relations. This involves communication of one form or another, be it ever so primitive. Object relations and communication are made possible through the close exchanges necessitated by the helplessness of the young and therefore limited to the altricials.

It is clearly evident that when Freud introduced the concept of the detour function into psychology—and his definition of thought as "experimental action" is a definition in terms of detour function—he was formulating a fundamental law of nature. In the form of the reality principle the detour function suspends action with the end result of a more efficient achievement of the instinct's aim. In *Beyond the Pleasure Principle* Freud touched on the evolutionary implications of the detour function; we are only now beginning to comprehend the scope of this law in phylogenesis. Thinking, a late acquisition in the course of phylogenesis, is such a detour, involving a delay in action in favor of achieving more efficient ultimate action. Communication, particularly of the allocentric kind, also requires the suspension of action.

On a more elementary level the progress achieved through the evolution of the altricials from the precocials consists again in a delay. Again it is action that is delayed; but now the delay is not interposed between the stimulus and the response to it. This time, achieving the capacity for action of any kind, regardless of the stimulus or of the urgency for action, is temporarily postponed in the ontogenetic development of the individual. While the precocial is born ready to spring into action, the young of the altricial have to undergo a prolonged period of learning and adaptation before they can proceed to act. The higher we go on the evolutionary

[26]

ladder, the more prolonged the delay necessary before goal-directed efficient action becomes available. This is particularly impressive in man. But when action finally does become available, it is incomparably more effective in the altricial than in the precocial in terms of the goals of the individual and their variability.

It is certain that evolution has combined in man some aspects of the precocial with most of the traits of the altricial. But the precocial aspects are limited to morphology; the congenital equipment and the behavior of the human young are essentially altricial, and to understand it more clearly we will examine nursing behavior in altricials.

Its earliest investigation goes back to Minkowski's (1916, 1922) studies beginning in 1916. They were later followed up by the already discussed work of Gamper (1926) and after him by the thorough neurologic investigations of Tilney and Casamajor (1924) and Tilney and Kubie (1931). Prechtl (1950, 1951, 1952), under the direction of Lorenz, performed the most recent and the most complete behavioral investigation of nursing behavior in altricials. The differences between the animals observed by them are minimal and not relevant for our particular purposes, and therefore we will summarize their description of the newborn kitten, which practically coincides with the findings of Kubie, Tilney, and Casamajor. We will refer at suitable points to some other mammals.

The experimental situation in which Prechtl observed his subjects was the following. Immediately after birth the kitten was placed on a horizontal smooth surface. In this situation the kitten performs rhythmical excursions of the head in the horizontal, in an arc of 180 degrees, at the average rate of fifteen per minute. While making these movements called by Prechtl and Schleidt (1950) "searching automatism," the animal crawls forward slowly in a circle. Tactile differences in the supporting surface, like dividing the surface in two parts, in one of which a cloth, in the other a cat fur is placed, provokes no change in the direction of the head movements or of the crawling. When, however, the two halves of the surface were covered on one side with a warm, on the other with a cold fur, the animals immediately turned their whole body toward the warm side.

If the kitten's path is obstructed by a wall with a narrow vertical cleft, no noticeable change in the reaction pattern occurs when the subject reaches it. But if the cleft in the same wall is made horizontal, the animal pushes itself into this cleft with its paddling movements. In our opinion, the effectiveness of the thermal stimulus and that of the horizontal cleft manifestly is based on the similarity with the nursing situation, in which the reclining warm mother animal forms a cleft with the supporting horizontal surface when nursing its young.

The same subjects were also observed in their normal nursing behavior with the mother animal. When the kitten reaches the mother animal, the searching automatism continues in an undirected manner until the nipple is found. It is not the nipple itself which is the key stimulus, but a naked skin area, not covered with fur. The response to this stimulus consists in the closing of the mouth around the nipple, the cessation of the searching automatism, and the beginning of the sucking movements. As described before regarding the nursing behavior of the human child, the behavior has two mutually exclusive patterns, the searching pattern on one hand, the orienting pattern or sucking on the other. I have found in the human newborn that when one of the two is functioning, it inhibits the other. This is an exact parallel of the mechanism operating in the orienting pattern as described by Gamper (1926).

In precocials the orientation in the searching automatism is completely different. A good example of this was described by Linn (1955) in a communication on "A Psychoanalytic Contribution to Comparative Neuropsychiatry." Newborn kids, lambs, calves walk toward any moving object that passes them. They will not turn aside for an obstacle but will push against the obstruction. When they encounter a wall, they orient themselves in a 45 degree angle to it, then edge along the wall, ending up with their heads pressing into a corner.

Even though we are trespassing on the preserves of animal ethologists, I think that we are in the position to explain the reasons why the searching automatism in precocials is different from that in altricials. The difference is determined (1) by the degree of maturation of the sensory modalities, and (2) by the degree of maturity of coordinated locomotion in the newborn. In the first place, precocials do not have to use thermal or tactile stimuli for their approach behavior. As seen from Linn's description, the releasing stimulus is a visual one, namely a moving object that passes the newborn. From the visual point of view, precocials are born more mature than altricials; their vision functions to the extent that they can respond to a moving object at a certain distance. Furthermore, their locomotion is also sufficiently developed to enable them to approach this object. That is not the case for altricials, in which neither vision nor locomotion is even distantly equal to perform such a feat.

In the second place, Prechtl's experiment has shown that the altricial kitten is oriented by the contact perception of a *horizontal* cleft. Precocials, however, who press with their heads into a corner of the wall obviously are oriented through

[29]

the stimulus of a *vertical* cleft, once they have made contact with an object.

The reason is obvious: the cat, being an altricial, has to adapt its nursing position to the helplessness of the kitten, to its incapacity to stand up during nursing and to reach upwards. Accordingly, the mother cat nurses lying next to the kittens. Her body forms a horizontal cleft with the supporting surface. As a result the horizontal cleft will become one of the orienting elements of the innate releasing mechanism[3] which leads the kitten to the teat. The precocial calf, however, nurses standing up and a vertical cleft is formed by the cow's body and hindleg; it is in the depth of this cleft that the udder is situated. Accordingly, the "pushing behavior" in the newborn precocial animal functions as a teat-seeking maneuver. Its function is the same as the searching behavior of the altricial, only in the altricial the cues are thermal and tactile, in the precocial visual and tactile.

Another aspect of the nursing behavior pattern is the activity of the forelimbs during sucking. Animal ethologists have remarked on the fact that altricials, in this case cats, dogs, guinea pigs, hamsters, push their forepaws alternately (very rarely simultaneously) forward, that is, against the udder of the mother animal. This behavior has been called *Milchtritt* in German; there is no English equivalent to this expression and I will call it with Tilney and Casamajor

[3] Innate Releasing Mechanism (IRM), a concept introduced by animal ethologists, has been defined by Tinbergen (1951) as follows: "There must be a special neurosensory mechanism that releases the reaction and is responsible for this selective susceptibility to a very special combination of sign stimuli. This mechanism we will call the Innate Releasing Mechanism (IRM)." A supplementary definition by Baerends (1950) reads: "The mechanism beginning at the sense organs, ending at the center released and including the sensitivity for the characteristics of the object, we will call the releasing mechanism."

[30]

(1924) "pressor movements."[4] They speak of the searching behavior and call it "crawling approach reaction." They state that the prehension of the mother animal's nipple by the kitten's mouth obviates the necessity of further crawling or further "cephalogyric" motions, head and body of the kitten becoming fixed in their special relations when the suctorial act begins. The two authors believe that impulses originating in the unfilled stomach and going to the vagal territory are the source of the afferent stimuli for both crawling approach and sucking reaction. They state that the *entire* motor response disappears only after the stomach is filled, and these impulses cease to flow. Some motor residue of the primitive paddling movements of the crawling approach persists after the young has become attached to the mother's teat. The residual paddling movements, adapted and determined by the motor complexes of sucking and swallowing, now become what the two authors call "the leg pressor movement of sucking." Tilney and Casamajor find this confirmed by the fact that also in the hindlegs there are slow synchronous movements, though less forceful and less regular in rhythm and excursion. Furthermore, they find it significant that these movements of the fore- and hindlimbs become less pronounced as the stomach becomes more completely filled.

The reader will readily realize the obvious parallels between the rooting behavior of the infant and that of the nonhuman mammalians of the altricial class.[5] The rooting

4 No attempt seems to have been made by animal ethologists to discover the physiological significance of this behavior, beyond voicing the opinion that it probably serves the purpose of a stimulus for milk secretion in the mother animal and is part of the total behavior complex of the nursing couple.

5 In my opinion a homologue to the pressor movements of the altricial cat can be clearly observed in the nursing behavior of the precocial calf. In the calf, however, the pressure is not exerted by the forelimbs. Instead, the suck-

behavior is unquestionably an archaic phylogenetically inherited behavior pattern, preformed at birth. Our main interest is what the human being makes out of this pattern. In the first place the rooting pattern very soon becomes efficiently organized and the nipple is centered in the mouth in one single snapping movement (Piaget, 1936; Brody, 1956). The motor patterns of the hands which accompany it and which at birth consisted of touching, pressing, clawing and scratching the breast, become organized into an increasingly rhythmical pattern well known to any mother who has nursed a baby. A kneading movement of the hand on the breast is developed and if the mother's hand and preferably finger is available, the baby's fingers after a month or two close around it and a game of rhythmically closing and opening is developed[6].

By the third or fourth week the child keeps his eyes open

---

ing calf repetitively butts the udder with its head. This behavior appears to have the same function as the residual movements of the kitten described by Tilney and Casamajor.

I think, furthermore, that the continuation of approach in the leg pressor movements of the kittens and in the butting behavior of the calf both are the manifestations of a much more general bio-psychological principle. This is the perseveration in a movement sequence, even after the goal, toward which the individual is striving, has been achieved. This functional perseveration of a behavior that has lost its purposive component is a characteristic of the undifferentiated phase in the human. It is in evidence whenever the integration of the personality is inadequate, either because it has not yet been achieved, or because a regression disrupts this integration. Accordingly, we can observe the phenomenon of perseveration not only in infants during and after the first year, but also in psychotic adults. We may speculate about its role in another one of the great laws of nature posited by Freud, namely the repetition compulsion.

6 On the other hand, the pressor movements during nursing are a confirmation of the close connection of mouth and hand in the human newborn, demonstrated by the investigations of Gamper (1926), on the psychological aspects of which I have elaborated elsewhere. It is worth adding to this that the searching behavior which leads to the pressor movements must be dependent on labyrinthine function. This is the third organ which I connected with mouth and hand in the above-mentioned context, the organ of which Minkowski proved that its function is demonstrable already in three-months-old fetuses.

[32]

during part of the nursing period and stares unwaveringly at the mother's face until he is satiated. I have discussed this behavior elsewhere (1954, 1955a), but wish to remind the reader that rooting behavior belongs to that stage of development at which neither consciousness nor perception in the commonly accepted sense of the term can be demonstrated. The appearance of rooting behavior immediately after birth, the history of its development in the fetus and its antecedents in phylogenesis show it to be an IRM in the sense in which ethologists defined the term. It is definitely not a volitional signal or a directed communication on the part of the child. It is an indicator, perceived by the environment as a signal and taken for a communication.

6.

Change of Function

We will now consider the three phenomena with which we are concerned from the point of view of their respective function. There is a clear-cut phenomenological similarity between the rooting behavior, the negative cephalogyric movements in the children suffering from hospitalism, and the semantic signal of the head-shaking "No."

In the course of tracing the origin of the rooting behavior in phylogenesis and in the fetal history of man, it has become evident that rooting is a behavior of turning toward, of approach, an appetitive[1] behavior (Glover, 1943), which has survival value for the newborn. In the terms of Freud's discussion (1925) of earliest behavior, it carries the meaning: "I want to take this into me"; it is a behavior of affirmation. In contrast to this, pathological negative cephalogyric movements in the deprived children definitely have the significance (though not the intended meaning) of refusal, of not wanting to take in, of negating.

Finally, the semantic signal of the head-shaking "No" also has the meaning of refusing and negating. Let me remind the reader that it is a much later development, appearing in the

[1] The term *appetitive* originates in scholastic philosophy and is based on Aristotle, who considered it an attribute of the drive. It was later taken up by Leibniz and introduced into psychoanalysis by Glover (1943), independently from its use in the 1930's by Leuba.

[34]

normal child after the fifteenth month of life, and that it is the result of an identification with the gesture of the child's libidinal object. Not only is the meaning of this last gesture a refusal, but it is important to remember that it is an intentionally directed semantic signal for the purpose of communicating this refusal to another person.

Rooting behavior, though phenomenologically similar, is not an intentional signal, nor a directed communication. It is the symptom of a striving toward the object, it is the indicator of the infant's need; its origin is not exteroceptive, which would be a response to an outer perception, but interoceptive, that is, a response to an inner experience. Thus two of the phenomenologically similar movements have a diametrically opposite significance: whereas the semantic signal of "No" represents a refusal, rooting represents a striving toward. Our investigation will have to elaborate how negative cephalogyric movements (the third related behavior pattern) are to be classified, for they are neither the one nor the other but seem to belong to a third category.

For this purpose we will have to begin with the rooting behavior and its significance. The rooting behavior in its specifically human aspect is provoked first by the tactile stimulation of the snout; somewhat later by the "change of position" stimulation of the vestibular organ. Under both circumstances the function of rooting is a turning toward the source of food; it is the counterpart—or perhaps it would be better to say, it is the outflow into motor action of a systemic need. I have the hunch, though as yet I cannot substantiate this with motion pictures or records of infants, that, even without stimulation, this rooting behavior will appear also when the infant is hungry. This is made probable by the observations of Tilney and Casamajor on cats and confirmed by observations on newborns and prematures made by

Prechtl and Klimpfinger. It is unquestionable that rooting behavior has the function of relieving a need and is the expression of this need. Or, in metapsychological terms: it is the expression of a tension and a striving toward tension discharge.

It is in these terms that we will try to understand the significance of the negative cephalogyric movements. Let us recall the circumstances under which they are manifested: the subjects in whom we observed the phenomenon were emotionally deprived infants who had been breast fed during the first three months of their lives. After this, emotional deprivation had progressively undermined their physical stamina, creating a picture of pathology described elsewhere (Spitz, 1945a). In this process their physical and psychological resources were rapidly declining and any stimulation was resented by them. We expressed the opinion that such stimulation, that the attempt to make contact with them, required them to abandon their lethargy and to use energy for a response. As they were husbanding their energies, they refused contact; the refusal took the form of negative cephalogyric movements.

We may advance the proposition that the attempt to make contact with these children results in a rise of tension in their system. Thereupon they try to reduce this tension by regressing—as they had regressed in every other respect all along the line—to the technique of tension reduction which they used in the first weeks of their lives: that method was rooting, that is rotating their head horizontally.

It is important to remember that this behavior is not directed to an object, but represents a regression to an objectless period. It is not a signal sent out to the object but a behavior calculated to relieve tension which stems from a period much earlier than that of true object relations.

[36]

That this behavior is phenomenologically identical with the much later semantic gesture of "No" appears to be a coincidence. It is this coincidence which tempts the adult onlooker to interpret these negative cephalogyric movements as a refusal of his approach or as negativism. But this is an adultomorphic interpretation. Far from being such a semantic gesture, cephalogyric movements are a regression to a stage in which directed communication is unimaginable.

It is noteworthy that on the road from rooting behavior to negative cephalogyric motion a change of function[2] occurs. For the onlooker the rooting baby seems to indicate that he is about to find gratification. Again for the onlooker, the cephalogyric child seems to manifest the opposite, namely his unpleasure, the discomfort of his tension. It would appear as if in the deprived children the movement would signify the opposite of what it signified in the rooting newborn. But this is only its appearance as seen from the angle of the onlooker. If we understand the two phenomena correctly, they signify the same, namely the seeking of discharge of tension, hunger tension in the rooting baby, tension caused by the disturbance of his quiescence in the cephalogyric baby.

2 "Change of function" is an explanatory concept derived from nineteenth-century social political theory on one hand, from biology on the other. In both cases it is an evolutionary concept with dynamic implications. It posits the combination of genetic continuity with relative functional independence in the case of social institutions. It was introduced into psychoanalytic thinking by Hartmann (1939, 1951, 1955). He considers it inherent in the structural point of view. Behavior originating in one sector of the personality will be used in the course of development in another sector and in a different function. He speaks of this as secondary autonomy and defines it in the same terms as the sociologists, namely, as a relative functional independence, despite genetic continuity. We will see a clear example of change of function in Chapter XI.

7.

Identification and Semantic Meaning

U P TO this point we have explored the differences and the similarities between negative cephalogyric movements and rooting behavior. We were able to discuss both phenomena in the terms of the undifferentiated phase of infant development, that is, in terms of their function. This is obvious for the rooting behavior, which is present only during the undifferentiated phase. For the negative cephalogyric movements it is equally valid, for we found that the negative cephalogyric movements are a regressive behavior, which also goes back to the undifferentiated phase. But from here on we will explore whether the head-shaking "No" stands in any relationship to these previously discussed two phenomena. In contradistinction to the phenomena of rooting behavior and of negative cephalogyric movements, the head-shaking "No" is a semantic signal which is achieved somewhere around the fifteenth month of life. Accordingly, the head-shaking "No" is governed by laws of a very different nature from those which rule either rooting behavior or negative cephalogyric movements. In a very general way one might say that rooting is governed by the Nirvana principle (that is, tension discharge), negative cephalogyric movements by the pleasure-unpleasure principle, while semantic head-shaking "No" conforms to the reality principle. For at the level of the head-shaking "No" semantic meaning has been achieved, and out of the undifferentiated phase the ego and the id have already differentiated from each other. Furthermore, a number of ego functions have been established and are operating within the ego itself.

The capacity to endow behavior with semantic meaning is one of these ego functions; moreover, we would be inclined to consider the attaching of semantic meaning to *gestures* in the same light as the attaching of meaning to verbal symbols.[1] Both the fixing of meaningful semantic gestures and of meaningful verbal symbols are linked with concept formation and with objectivation in the child's development (Hartmann, 1947, 1951). Capacity to endow gesture and sound production with meaning thus acquires the role of an ego apparatus. Therefore the dimension which will orient our new line of investigation is that of semantic meaning.

To begin with, we will ask ourselves whether it is a mere coincidence that the pathological negative cephalogyric movements (which one can observe in deprived children around the ninth month of their lives) are phenotypically similar to the movements used in the semantic gesture of the head-shaking "No" of the fifteen- to eighteen-months-old normal child. Is there really no connection between the two?

We may find an answer to this question if we examine how each of these two phenomena, negative cephalogyric movements on the one hand and head-shaking "No" on the other, came into being. We have seen in the preceding chapters that

---

1 Freud (1905b) expressed this idea from a somewhat different viewpoint, as follows: "Indeed, I can imagine that bodily innervation which is consensual to the idea conceived is the beginning and origin of mimicry for purposes of communication. For, in order to be in a position to serve this purpose, it is only necessary to increase it and make it conspicuous to the other."

[39]

the negative cephalogyric movements represent something in the nature of an ego regression to the rooting behavior. Actually it is questionable whether we can already speak of an ego (in the commonly accepted sense of the word) in the deprived children. But in view of the fact that regression is an extremely primitive mechanism which operates even on the physiological level, it is immaterial whether in the case of these infants an ego is involved or not.

Semantic head-shaking denegation is a behavior of a very different order. It certainly is not the result of a regression, but represents progress. It is a behavior in which the infant attaches to a gesture an ideational content which is meaningful to his environment. In achieving this semantic meaning, the defense mechanism of identification is used in an adaptive role. Observation shows that semantic head-shaking, the negation, is acquired in identification with the adult's gesture.

Identification and Imitation

Identification and imitation have been widely and conflictingly discussed in psychoanalytic literature. In achieving semantic meaning, the two play a conspicuous role and we will therefore have to discuss them at greater length. We will disregard the problem of primary identification; that concept can only be applied at the undifferentiated stage. At the stage at which semantic meaning is acquired, the boundaries between the "I" and the "non-I" have already been established for quite a while, and any identification which takes place is of a higher order of complexity.

The prestages of identification become manifest in the child's early gesture identification, a concept introduced by Berta Bornstein. They appear after the sixth month of life, partly in the form of straightforward imitation and partly in more advanced forms. Among the latter are those in which the child appears to conform with the libidinal object's attitudes. The semantic head-shaking "No" is a much later acquisition, it appears after the fifteenth month of life.

Identification with the gesture, as well as the subsequent manifestations of identification, will play a conspicuous role in the learning processses of the child. We mostly become aware of them when the child imitates actions which are meaningful to the grownup but are not meaningful to the child. Similarly, we are greatly impressed when the child repeats words which to him must be completely meaningless.

We may note here that few of us are aware of the fact that it is not only the child who imitates the grownup, but that the obverse is also the case. This is a phenomenon which to my knowledge has never been investigated either in its general or in its specific aspect. Yet it plays a significant role in the formation and development of object relations both from the viewpoint of the parent and from that of the child.

When the parents imitate the little child's gesture or words, they have to perform an identification on a very primitive level. This is a level which usually is inaccessible to the adult because of infantile amnesia. Trespassing on this territory becomes permissible only because the parents perform this temporary regression in the interest of the child. Therefore this identification becomes permissible from the social viewpoint and from that of the superego.

Indeed, these parental identificatory processes are part and parcel of object relations. Without them the development of the child into a human being would be impeded. I think we may say without exaggeration that these parental identifications on an archaic level form a bridge with the help of which the child, reversing the process, becomes able to identify with the parent. The parent's identifications—we may remind the reader that identification is an unconscious process—with infantile actions, feelings, desires have indubitably a constructive role. Nevertheless, a certain amount of guilt attaches to the public display of this temporary regression by the parents. That becomes manifest in the "humorous" derision shown by many for the "boring" parents who tell "cute" stories about their children. The humor, the mockery and the boredom are defenses against being seduced into all too familiar and forbidden archaic territory.

For the child the situation appears more unproblematic. Imitations by the parents indubitably reinforce his identifications and, concomitantly, the learning process. It is true that the interplay of parental and child aggression may sometimes also transform this particular relation into a frustrating one. The individual history of the child will determine the role played by these mutual imitations. But whether or not parental imitation reinforces the child's own gesture and word imitation, the exchanges involved in the mutual imitation of gesture and word have a powerful effect on the progressive unfolding of the child's personality.

Imitation of and identification with the gesture are one of the child's major contributions to the formation of object relations. The first identifications with parental gestures appear in the third and fourth quarter of the first year and are echo-like reproductions of the adult's gesture. They arise in the course of the unfolding object relations, mostly as games, between the adult and the infant, as an immediate response, mirroring a gesture initiated by the adult. In the next phase the child takes the initiative; imitations of behavior observed in the libidinal object are placed by the child into the service of his spontaneous actions and games, even in the absence of the adult. That identification proper is at work in this performance is evident; the infant has incorporated into the memory system of his ego actions observed in the libidinal object, and as a result a modification of the ego's structure has taken place.

Prohibitions and Commands

On the age level of nine to twelve months at which primitive gesture identification develops, the child also acquires the first understanding of commands and prohibitions. In the nature of things, prohibitions are vastly more numerous at this age than commands. They are expressed by the grownup mostly verbally and given emphasis by appropriate gestures, like finger-wagging and head-shaking. Erect locomotion, which is also acquired at this age, rapidly increases the child's autonomy, and concomitantly such prohibitions as the "No, No" of the grownup will become more and more frequent in more and more varied situations.

In this way the child's first dim understanding of prohibitions will be experienced and re-experienced in the exchanges between the child and the grownup. The memory traces of these experiences accumulate in ever-increasing numbers in the course of the subsequent months.

For our present purposes, we can consider each experience of prohibition as consisting of two parts: one is the act (of the child) which is prohibited; the second the adult's prohibiting behavior (nonverbal and verbal). The child's act, the material circumstances in which it takes place, the child's intentions toward these, vary from occasion to occasion. The adult's prohibition remains qualitatively invariant, be the occasions ever so dissimilar.

The invariance of the "No" gesture and word within multiform experiences would tend to insure a lasting memory

[43]

trace through the cumulative effect of repetition.[2] This is a mechanical explanation which we find unsatisfactory. Two considerations, one based on experiment, the other on psychoanalytic theory, give a better and more instructive insight into the process leading to the singling out of the "No" as a permanent memory trace.

The Gestalt Thesis

The first is a finding of Gestalt psychology. In an experiment which has become a classic, Zeigarnik (1927) proved that uncompleted actions are better recalled than completed ones. If we consider the problem of the adult's prohibiting "No" in the light of Zeigarnik's findings, it becomes obvious that for the child each prohibition, be it verbal, be it by gesture or be it a combination of both, inhibits an action initiated by the child. The growing number of prohibitions, therefore, leaves in their wake an equal number of uncompleted "tasks." Their common element, the "No," the prohibiting gesture and word, thus is enabled to become the invariant factor remembered, out of an accumulation of uncompleted "tasks."

A Psychoanalytic Proposition

The second, the psychoanalytic approach, starts out with the consideration that each prohibition involves a frustration. Whether we prohibit the child's activity, or make it impossible for the child to get something which he desires, or whether we disagree with the form which he wishes to give to his object relations, we will always be frustrating his id drives. Therefore, the memory traces of the prohibitions, the

2 William James (1890), speaking of abstractions, states: "What is associated now with one thing and now with another tends to become dissociated from either and to grow into an object of abstract contemplation by the mind. One might call this the law of dissociation by varying concomitants" (p. 506).

gestures and words in which we express them, will be endowed
with a specific affective cathexis, with the feeling tone of
refusal, of defeat, of bafflement, of being thwarted—in one
word, of frustration. It is this very specific affective charge
which ensures the permanence of the memory trace of the
prohibiting "No," be it gesture or word.

Though these two considerations throw some light on our
problem, psychoanalytic insight has more to contribute to its
understanding. Prohibitions, by interrupting the child's activity, invite a return to passivity. This is a regressive step in
the direction of the narcissistic organization of the ego. But
at the age when prohibitions come to be effective, the child
is progressing from the narcissistic stage to the stage of object
relations. He will not readily let himself be forced back into
passivity (Freud, 1931; Anna Freud, 1952), but will attempt
to overcome the obstacles in the path of his progress. However, the motive force of his efforts is not limited only to the
biological urge to progress from passivity to activity. A dynamic factor is added to this, for the affective charge of the
frustration experience provokes an aggressive cathexis from
the id with which the memory trace of the prohibition will
be invested.

Impelled by these forces, and in an attempt to master the
situation, the child makes use of a defense mechanism. At the
end of the first year of life and throughout the second year
the most conspicuous adaptive device, applied in practically
every situation requiring mastery or defense, is the mechanism of identification. In this case, a particular form of
identification will be used.

Already in 1926 and 1931 Freud, in "On Female Sexuality," outlined a conspicuous form of behavior in the child.
This behavior plays an important role in the child's efforts
to master both his own capacities and the outside world. As

[45]

Freud puts it: "It is easy to observe how, in every field of psychical experience . . . an impression passively received evokes in children a tendency to an active response. They try to do themselves what has just been done to them. This is part of their task of mastering the outside world and may even lead to their endeavoring to repeat impressions which they would have good reason to avoid because of their disagreeable content."

Anna Freud (1936) recognized that the adaptive behavior described by Freud can be, and frequently is, used for the purpose of defense and constitutes one of the important defense mechanisms. She called it the defense mechanism of "identification with the aggressor."

Anna Freud illustrates this defense mechanism with the help of a series of cases, some at the oedipal level, some older. The conflict involved is essentially one between external objects and the ego. Through identification with the aggressor, however, the conflict is internalized; thus we may assume that in all these cases the superego, or at least its immediate precursors begin to operate.

The fifteen-months-old who acquires the "No" gesture from the adult also does so as a result of the conflict between his ego and an external object. However, no superego is present at this stage; the libidinal object is at the same time the authority whose introjected imago is destined to be transformed into the superego years later. We therefore do not have to consider the role of the superego in our present discussion of the acquisition of the "No" gesture. There is one further difference which we believe to be more apparent than real. Anna Freud speaks of the "aggressor," and we of the "frustrator." The difference, I think, is only in emphasis.

The dynamics which lead to the acquisition of the semantic "No" appear to us to be the following. The libidinal ob-

[46]

ject's "No" inflicts a frustration on the child and causes unpleasure. Thereupon the "No" (word and gesture) is laid down as a memory trace in the ego's memory system. In the id, the affective charge of unpleasure, separated from this presentation, will call forth an aggressive cathexis which is now attached by way of association to the memory trace in the ego.

When the child identifies with the libidinal object "he passes from the passivity of the experience to the activity of the game" (Freud, 1920, p. 17). In the words of Anna Freud (1936, p. 125), ". . . identification with the aggressor is succeeded by the active assault on the outside world."

The "No" (gesture and word) is the identificatory link with the libidinal object. In virtue of the aggressive cathexis with which the "No" has been endowed in the process of the numerous unpleasure experiences connected with this memory trace, it becomes the suitable vehicle to express aggression. The "No" is a device used to express the aggression in the defense mechanism of identification with the aggressor. The aggressor in this case is the frustrating object against whom his own "No" is hurled; in the words of Freud (1931): "it [the child] does really make the mother the object in relation to which it assumes the role of the active subject." We will return to the interesting aspect of the shift of cathectic investment of the memory trace from unpleasure to aggression.

In her further discussion of the mechanism, Anna Freud shows that identification with the aggressor represents a preliminary phase of the superego. This is quite evident in the course of the second year of life, for the child who has acquired the semantic "No" turns this device also against himself (Howe, 1955). This particular aspect of intracommunication (Cobliner, 1955) does not belong in the framework of our present study. But we will mention in passing that ob-

[47]

servers of children's play are familiar with the role-playing child in the second year of life who says or gestures "No, No" toward himself. Obviously he has assumed the mother's role. We believe that this is the earliest example of what Anna Freud (1952) has described with the words: "The child . . . adopts the mother's role . . . thus playing 'mother and child' with his own body." Furthermore, it is at the same time a preliminary phase of superego development, as described by her in *The Ego and the Mechanisms of Defense.*

Our observations of children at the age when they begin to identify show that there is a definite urge to identify with the love object at all costs. The urge to identify is so strong, it plays such a major role in the object relations, that the child identifies indiscriminately with whatever behavior of the love object he is able to appropriate. It is as if identification went through a phase of nondifferentiation. It is indulged in by the child for identification's sake, is used for object relations and mastery, for defense and attack. Perhaps the indiscriminateness in appropriating everything that is available from the love object—things, gestures, inflexions, actions, attitudes, etc.—explains the origin of the identification with the aggressor.[3] If the child identifies for identifica-

[3] We believe that the sudden mushrooming of both imitation and identification in this particular phase of infancy can be explained by a very general law of development. We refer to the findings of McGraw (1935), according to which any behavior pattern has an initial phase in which it can be recognized, a second phase in which it proliferates, so that the activity itself becomes the incentive for repetition, and a third phase in which the exaggeration of this particular movement becomes checked or inhibited by the emergence of others. In our opinion, this law applies not only to behavior patterns but also to the acquisition of new psychological functions, in this case to a mechanism of defense. In the phase to which we refer, a major part of the child's object relations takes the form of identification. It goes without saying that these identifications will be selective ones. The increased use of identification by the child corresponds to the phase of proliferation in McGraw's sequence. In a later phase the tendency to identify at all costs will recede and be replaced by other psychic processes.

tion's sake with anything the love object does, then he will identify also with what causes him unpleasure. Once this pattern is laid down and has followed through a certain period of development, it will become established, because it turns out to be a useful one in many aspects.

Conditions Governing the Selectivity in Identification

However, it appears desirable to be more specific about what the child takes over when he identifies with the aggressor. In the innumerable other identifications he tries to appropriate everything from the love object. Yet each individual child obviously makes a selection of his own among the vast number of items which he could take over from the grown-ups surrounding him. To my knowledge nothing has been published on the conditions which govern his selection. It is obvious that some of the principles governing this selection must derive from the personal emotional history of each individual child.

But we also believe that there exist more general principles for this process and that some of them become evident in the fifteen-months-old in the specific instance of identifications with the aggressor. One such general principle refers to the question of what the fifteen-months-old is able to take over from the love object in virtue of the limitations of his own psychic organization. These limitations will determine the way he can deal with what is made available to him by the love object.

Among the various psychological and physical components which constitute the love object's frustrating action, we can distinguish three. They are the object's behavior, the mental processes and contents of which the behavior is an expression, and the affects which underly and accompany this behavior. The child deals differently with each of them.

[49]

The fifteen-months-old's psychic equipment enables him readily to perceive and distinguish diacritically the object's physical behavior. Accordingly, in his identification, he will appropriate this component fairly exactly. We will refrain, both here and in what follows, from any extensive discussion of the question of how much of this input will be processed by the child, how it is processed and when.

On the other hand, the adult's mental processes and the possible rational reasons for his "No" are completely beyond the fifteen-months-old's capacities of understanding. He cannot understand whether the adult prohibits because of concern for the child's safety or because of anger when the child does something forbidden. At this age the child does not yet think in rational categories, and ignores the laws of cause and effect. For this reason, as well as because of his lack of insight into the processes going on in another person, he is not capable of empathy in the commonly accepted sense of the term.

Regarding the third component, the affects underlying the adult's frustrating behavior, the situation is again different. It appears from my observations that the child in the second year still has only a global perception of his partner's affects. This level of perception of affects is comparable to the global *sensory* perception of the three-months-old. Just as the three-months-old slowly develops diacritic discrimination of sensory stimuli in the course of the first year, the older child will (much more slowly and over many years) develop a discrimination of the various affects perceived in others and of their reason.

For the beginning of the second year of life I am inclined to assume that the child distinguishes in the adult partner two affects only. I will call them the affect "for" and the affect "against." In our usual terms, the child feels either that the love object loves him or that the love object hates him.

This lack of discrimination in the child can be clearly demonstrated in motion pictures. That is shown very impressively in Priv. Case No. 2 (age 0; 11 + 24).

> The observer is playing a game with the child and offers him a toy. After the child has taken possession of the toy and played with it, the observer takes the toy away again. When the child reaches for the toy, the observer wags his finger, shakes his head and says: "No, no." Notwithstanding the smiling, friendly expression of the observer, Priv. No. 2 hastily draws back his hand, and sits with downcast eyes and an expression of embarrassment and shame as if he had done something terrible.

This child, at the age of eleven months and twenty-four days, clearly understands the prohibition. At the same time he misinterprets the prohibiting adult's affect in a global manner: "You are not *for* me; therefore you are *against* me." We will disregard here the implications contained in Priv. No. 2's facial expression which shows that the love object is against him when he has done something wrong. Three or four months later, we may expect him to be able to take over the prohibiting gesture from the adult.

In identifying with the "No" gesture, the child takes over from the adult the diacritically perceived sensory data of the head-shaking gesture and "No" word. But the affect still will be perceived only globally as "against." This affect "against" together with the gesture will be taken over in the identification with the aggressor when the child experiences unpleasure because of a demand of the adult. If on this occasion the experiencing of unpleasure and of the affect "against" generates a thought process in the child, it will be all his own and certainly not taken over from the aggressor.

[51]

The identification with the aggressor in the "No" gesture therefore remains limited to the imitation of the physical action, and to the appropriation of the global quality of the affect; the two are then turned against the aggressor. Simultaneously thought processes are triggered in the child. All three together—imitation, turning of the affects against the adult, thought process—represent energy transformations on a large scale. This energy transformation is a step forward in the domestication of the drives, as a result of the ever-growing closeness of object relations. In this transformation of energies the motor expression of the affect "against" has been subjected to the control of the ego and modified, with far-reaching consequences of which we will speak later. For the time being, we must return to our primary concern, the question of how the child through an identification with the aggressor takes over the head-shaking "No," and what this represents both from the viewpoint of thought processes and from that of psychic structure.

Thought Processes and Psychic Structure

From the viewpoint of the thought processes a significant development has been initiated when the child indicates a decision in the form of refusal through head-shaking. The use of this gesture is the manifest evidence of a judgment at which the child has arrived. When the child expresses this particular judgment, he also discloses that he has acquired the capacity to perform the mental operation of negation. That in turn inevitably will lead to the formation of the abstract concept underlying the negative, the first abstract concept to appear in mentation. But of this later.

Structurally, from the viewpoint of the id, a shift from passivity to activity has taken place and a new avenue for the discharge of aggression has been created. From the viewpoint

[52]

of the ego, the changes are more numerous and more evident; we will only point out a few of them. The dynamics inherent in the identificatory process were set in motion under the pressure of the repetitive frustrations and through the efforts to overcome these. We will show in what follows that the ego has now acquired a method of dealing both with the environment and with the self—a method which hitherto had not been available.

This is a major step in the child's progress from initial helplessness and complete dependence to an ever-increasing autonomy. The application of the capacity of judgment in his dealings with the surround on one hand, in his dealings with himself on the other, leads to a progressive objectivation of mental processes. Another of these changes is that the radius of object relations has been expanded. Previously physical resistance was used in unpleasure situations. Now refusal can be expressed without involving action, and with this newly acquired autonomy the period of stubbornness can begin.

Shift from Passivity to Activity

Of course, the question of the child's increasing autonomy should also be considered from the viewpoint of his shift from passivity to activity. The first major step in active social behavior is the infant's smiling response. From there on the unfolding of activity is rapid and follows closely the lines of somatic achievements until the appearance of the second major step, the eight-months anxiety. Its advent presumably marks the turning point at which an extensive proliferation of mental activity begins; it will accompany the equally powerful increase of physical activity characteristic of this age, which is made possible by the maturation of musculature and by the development of muscular coordination.

In this spectacular increase of mental and physical activity we might be tempted to consider the appearance of the eight-months anxiety as a first manifestation of negation, since it is a refusal of the stranger's approach. However, nothing in this behavior justifies us to consider it more than an unpleasure manifestation, combined with withdrawal. It certainly has the meaning of refusal, but it is far from having achieved the dignity of the head-shaking "No" gesture. With the latter the child manifests his identification with the grownup's prohibition; that, however, is an abstractive performance.

The eight-months anxiety is a much simpler performance; the sequence is as follows. The child produces first a scanning behavior, namely the seeking for the lost love object, the mother. A decision is now made by the function of judgment "whether something which is present in the ego as an image, can also be re-discovered in perception" (Freud, 1925). The realization that it cannot be rediscovered in the given instance provokes a response of unpleasure. In terms of the eight-months anxiety, what we observe can be understood as follows: the stranger's face is compared to the memory traces of the mother's face and found wanting. This is not mother, she is still lost. Unpleasure is experienced and manifested. This is a process which requires no abstraction, nor does it require a process of identification—at least not in the restricted sense in which we have used the term to describe how the child acquires gestures and words through identification with the grownup.

It may clarify the difference between the processes involved in the manifestation of the eight-months anxiety and those in the semantic gesture of denegation if we take a closer look at some behavioral aspects of the eight-months anxiety. The eight-months-old's response to the stranger covers quite a gamut; it can go from an expression of awe, or lowering the eyes as if embarrassed, or covering the eyes with the hands, or lifting the clothing before the eyes, to hiding the face in the blankets, etc. With the exception of the first and mildest form, all these actions serve to exclude the perception of the stranger's face. In other terms, they are a "denial in act" (Anna Freud, 1936), a prestage of defense. It is an attempt to avoid the task of reality testing in a situation in which this task is painful. It is also a step forward from the earlier method used, namely that of primitive repression. Instead of withdrawing the cathexis from the perception of the unpleasant (an id process), an action is performed (by the ego) to exclude perception. This action is conscious and intentional. The best proof that the child is fully conscious of what he is doing, but still tries in a wishful way to make the stranger disappear, is that the child looks back at the stranger again and again. He peeks between his fingers, he lifts his face from the blanket—and hides it again.

Something of this indecision, of this wavering, of this conflict is carried over into negation also. This is not surprising, for ambivalence will accompany the child's development for a long time to come, throughout the second year and more. We do find the child signifying his refusal by gesture or word, yet at the same time doing what he seems to refuse. But this is a phenomenon of a different order.

Once the child can express negation by gesture or word, he has left behind him the illusory attempts at denial; identification with the aggressor will lead him to signify his own refusal by adopting the adult's "No" gesture for this purpose. This necessitates, as we have already stated, a shift from the passive to the active role; it is more than just a shift, it involves also something else.

Up to this point, in the identification through the gesture, the child consciously sided *with* the adult and endeavored "to do as he does." But when, with the help of unconscious processes, the child succeeds in attaching semantic meaning to the "No" gesture and takes it over from the love object, he becomes able to use it *against* the adult.

In terms of analytic theory, we have been able to distinguish within the sequence leading to the achievement of the head-shaking "No" the following elements: memory traces are laid down in the course of a series of affective experiences; the affective nature of these experiences in its turn will call forth successive attempts at identification with the prohibiting grownup. The result of this identificatory process is that in consequence of the affect charges proceeding from the id, a change in the child's ego takes place. This change becomes manifest, on one hand, in the child's personality as an increase of autonomy which enables the child to signify refusal spontaneously through the adoption of the adult's gesture. On the other, the shift of forces set in motion results in the reintegration of the child's thought processes on a higher level, namely on that of a beginning capacity of abstraction.

One feels inclined to speculate whether this extraordinary new achievement has been made possible through the process discussed on pages 45-47 and 52. We described how unpleasure (because of frustration) provoked a thrust of aggression which was attached to the memory trace of the "No." *Pari passu,* a change from passivity to activity takes place on the id level in the process of acquiring the "No."

In the ego, on the other hand, a large-scale restructuration becomes noticeable. That is evidenced through the fact that the child becomes able to sever ties surviving from primary narcissistic dependent relations. These are the ties with the person who is destined to become eventually the libidinal object. They persist during the subsequent development of anaclitic object relations, while the libidinal object still remained the external part of the ego. The consequences of being able to turn the "No" against the libidinal object, against what had only recently been the need-gratifying motor executive of the child's ego, are: (1) a becoming aware of the separateness of the self from the object; (2) a far-reaching enrichment of the child's object relations. The enrichment takes place in various other aspects also and we will return to them in a later chapter.

The indicator that the child has achieved the measure of abstraction necessary to signify refusal spontaneously is his use of the head-shaking "No" or of the word "No." It indicates that the reiterated "No" of the grownup has been synthesized into a negation by the child and that the child has appropriated negation for his own mental operations.

Abstraction

The concept of abstraction is not the topic of the present study. However, a few remarks appear in order to elucidate the cathectic shifts which take place when the infant becomes able to perform this decisive step in intellectual development. In the course of identifying with the aggressor, passive submission to unpleasure was replaced by activity, culminating in the attachment of aggressive cathexis to the presentation of the "No." This restructuration in the distribution of psychic energy at the same time produces the capacity for abstraction, a mode of mentation until then not available to the child.

We want to stress that abstraction is not acquired through identification with the adult, though the head-shaking "No" *is* thus acquired. Abstraction is never the result of an identification; it is an autonomous achievement of the synthetic activity of the ego. Elements considered inessential by the subject are detached from the experiential referent with the help of aggression.[4] Concomitantly the elements considered essential are synthesized into a symbolic representation of the experiential referent. The symbolic representation subsequently becomes a generalized concept. With its help the familiar can be rediscovered in the unfamiliar. We have previously given an example of this process when we described the mechanical dissociation of the love object's "No" from the occasions on which the "No" is used (pp. 43-44).

In this description of abstraction we have availed ourselves of the genetic and of the dynamic as well as of the structural approach. Our conclusions are very close to those of Rapaport (1951), as well as to those of Inhelder (1956). Rapaport deals with abstraction in the framework of his study of thinking and concludes that abstraction is based on the mechanism of isolation, thus emphasizing the role of the defense mechanism. Inhelder, who speaks of abstraction on the basis of direct child observation and experiment, describes abstraction as the capacity of the child to represent and schematize experiences with the help of symbols and signs which are detached from the actual givens.

We have assumed that this process is accelerated through the fact that each prohibition of the adult represents a frustration for the child. The frustration inhibits the discharge of a tension which will then seek its outlet in another "path of discharge" (Freud, 1895a, p. 379)—in our present

[4] The distinction between essential and nonessential elements is made on affective grounds and not for cognitive reasons. Thus in the acquisition of the "No" the essential element is the emotional frustration by the love object and not the particular situation, e.g., the candy which the child tries to reach or the boiling coffeepot he tries to upset. The affective frustration by the love object is always more essential than the subordinate goal of getting the candy or reaching the coffeepot. The essential quality of affective frustration by the love object singles out, among all the other possibilities of abstraction, the "No" and makes it the first abstract concept of mentation.

[58]

case, this outlet is destined eventually to become an instrument of communication. The child's head-shaking "No" is the visible proof of his identification with the grownup; at the same time it initiates the era of allocentric communication.

Our attempt to establish a connection between the semantic head-shaking "No" on one hand, pathological cephalogyric movements and rooting on the other, has led us far afield. We have gained some insight into the earliest beginnings of allocentric communication. However, neither the semantic meaning nor the dynamics involved in the acquisition of the head-shaking "No" have provided us with any direct link to the earlier manifestations. We will therefore have to consider some further aspects in the development of earliest object relations before we can attempt to answer our question.

8.

Object Relations and Communication

I<small>N THE</small> preceding chapter we have attempted to clarify from the structural, genetic and dynamic viewpoints the manner in which the child endows gesture and word with meaning. At the same time we traced the role played by identification in this process. Let us now visualize in concrete terms the behavior of which we are speaking.

Mother has placed Johnny in a high chair and prepares to feed him. She brings a bowl of mashed carrots. As soon as he sees them from afar, Johnny, who had eaten his porridge with enthusiasm, begins shaking his head violently, to the accompaniment of vocalization expressing displeasure. Mother responds, and with endearments and encouraging words tries to overcome the child's refusal.

This trivial little episode calls our attention to the fact that this interchange has some obvious aspects, with which we have not yet dealt and which we will now proceed to examine. In the first place, a communication, nonverbal from the child's side, verbal from the mother's side, has taken place between the two. It is clear that each of them understands the message coming from the other, that they have tacitly reached an agreement on the code they are using. The particular form which their code of communication has taken is the result of the history of the object relations between Johnny and his mother. We must therefore turn our attention to the role of object relations in achieving communication.

Usually the psychoanalyst studies object relations in terms of libidinal phases. In the present monograph we are precluded from doing this since the period under study embraces hardly more than the oral stage. On the other hand, though object relations are also the major point of interest in psychoanalytic therapy, the therapist views them through the eyes of a single individual, the patient. In therapy, the essential reciprocity of object relations shows up primarily in the form of transference and countertransference. In our present genetic study of the relations leading to communication we will endeavor to keep in mind that the object relations we are investigating have to be understood in terms of the reciprocity within the dyad formed by the infant and the libidinal object.

At the same time it should be remembered that when we examine structure, dynamics, identification in one chapter, object relations in another, we are not suggesting that they are separate from each other within the personality. They form an indivisible totality, they are interdependent, interacting, and any apparent separateness derives from the observer, that is from the different angles from which he considers one and the same phenomenon. We have implied as much in our exploration of the dynamics which operate in the achievement of semantic meaning.

We will subdivide our discussion on the role of object relations in the establishment of semantic communication into a general and into a clinical part (Chapter IX), and then summarize our conclusions from the latter.

[61]

Communication and Object Relations

We have stated that rooting is received by the mother as a communication but is not a communication from the viewpoint of the child, for rooting behavior takes place at the objectless stage. It is not purposive behavior. It is a physiologically inbuilt pattern which has a function, but no subjective purpose. The function is that of ensuring the survival of the individual by re-establishing the connection with the food dispenser which was interrupted through the severing of the umbilical cord. This function is a physiological one; it recedes rapidly with maturation. It is our belief, however, that it is a prototype behavior which reappears a year later within the framework of object relations, when it will be endowed with psychic content and used as a device for communication.

This elaboration of rooting has a parallel in that of the grasping pattern (Spitz, 1951). At birth grasping is a skin and tendon reflex which recedes with the progressive maturation of the child. Only when its reflex quality has been lost, can it be psychologically invested and used as purposive grasping. It reappears in pathological processes as forced grasping; similarly the rooting pattern reappears in the pathological condition of the emotionally deprived children.

The reader will recall that already Gamper (1926), but also Tilney and Casamajor (1924), had divided rooting behavior into two parts, each with a different motor pattern. The first was called by Gamper the "oral orientation reflex," a scanning behavior; we consider this rooting proper. The second is the prehension of the stimulus by the lips, a consummatory behavior, which is preceded by the preparatory behavior of rooting proper.[1] We believe that from the psycho-

1 See footnote 2 below.

[62]

logical point of view it is important to make a clear distinction not only between the motor patterns of these two behaviors, but also between their subsequent fate. We have seen in the preceding paragraph that rooting proper undergoes a process of involution and disappears from the inventory of the infant's behavior patterns. It is discontinued and reappears only after a long interruption. In contrast to this, the development of the prehension pattern of the lips, the clinging, is uninterrupted; its development is continuous.

In our opinion, the clinging behavior of the lips around the nipple, later the clinging of hands and fingers on the breast, are the precursors and prototypes of object relations. This clinging behavior is carried forward uninterruptedly in a variety of modifications, not only throughout the first and second year, but practically throughout life. The proverbial "clinging to mother's apron string" is more than a picturesque form of speech.

The play of hand and fingers on the breast is one of the many early forms of reciprocity between mother and child. There can be no doubt that it is perceived by the mother as an early form of communication, as signals on a very elementary level. These signals are sent out by the nursing infant; at this stage they are neither purposive nor directed, they take place simply as a function of inner processes which find their discharge in muscular action (Tilney and Casamajor, 1924). In its most obvious aspect this muscular action consists in the rhythmic hand contractions of the baby. Less obvious but ever present is the squirming of the baby's body and the movements of his legs; not obvious to the observer at all, but obvious to the mother, is the baby's mouth activity on the nipple, the sucking, licking, biting activity.

And we should not overlook the fact that the hungry baby's vocalizations before the feeding, be it screaming, whimpering, wailing, also act as signals which the mother receives and perceives on two levels: (1) the conscious cognitive level, on which she reacts by taking the baby up, nursing it, adjusting her position, etc., and (2) the unconscious level, on which her affects and autonomous functions are mobilized.

Of this unconscious response I had a most convincing proof when observing two mothers with their babies. One of them, Mary, had weaned her baby a few days earlier. The other, Jane, was still nursing hers and had it next to her in a baby carriage. The two women were talking to each other when Jane's baby began getting restless and with screams rapidly increasing in volume indicated his desire for nursing. Jane started making preparations to nurse him, while the impatient baby continued screaming more and more lustily. At this moment two wet spots appeared on the blouse of Mary, indicating that the baby's communication had set her autonomous function in motion and that she was responding by secreting milk, although she had stopped nursing several days ago.

The two levels on which the mother receives and perceives the nursing communications are clearly evident in this example. The role played by the mother's unconscious attitudes toward *having* a child (in general) and toward her *own* child's individuality in particular can hardly be overrated for her relation to her child. One of the most drastic illustrations of this is a personal communication to me by a woman who had been an inmate of a Nazi concentration camp.

She told me that the camp's doctor, himself a fellow inmate, had said to her that there were no breast-feeding problems in the concentration camp, and that every mother had milk. He felt that this was so because the mothers knew that if breast feeding was not forthcoming, the camp authorities would let the baby die of inanition.

[64]

It is clear that the mother's response to the nonvolitional messages from the newborn, as described above, can go wrong on either of the two levels mentioned, the conscious and the unconscious level, or on both. However, this is a problem which goes beyond the framework of our present study. It is the problem of the mother's capacity to create conditions making it possible for the child to establish object relations, and of the extent to which her individual psychopathology limits this capacity.

We will now consider the child's role in establishing the earliest precursors of object relations. We mentioned already that rooting in its early phylogenetic form is a scanning behavior. It is of interest to note that rooting as a *scanning* behavior has a relatively subordinate role: it leads to the *consummatory* act of introducing the nipple into the mouth.[2] The scanning activity provides no immediate instinctual gratification. One may say that phylogenetically it fulfills an anticipatory role which has the character of a detour leading to eventual need gratification. Rooting will soon be abandoned and the tactile (proximity) searching will be replaced by visual (distance) perception. This is another mode of scanning, destined eventually to become the prototype of mental activity.

In contradistinction to rooting, the clinging of the lips, of hand and fingers, will be carried on in an unbroken line into the object relations themselves. The actions of the mouth achieve the immediate gratification of the instinct. Therefore, in the beginning at least, mouth actions do not lend themselves as well for the purposes of communication

---

2 We are indebted to Mortimer Ostow (1955) for the clear separation of consummatory techniques from scanning and searching techniques, as well as to Kubie (1956) for his further differentiation of the behavior patterns into anticipatory, supportive, appetitive and consummatory behavior.

[65]

as rooting. Communication is a detour function, and immediate need gratification does not favor the development of detour functions.

Rooting, however, originally is, and also remains in its further development, a detour behavior motivated by the need to discharge the tension caused by the instinct and is not in itself a direct need gratification. Thus in the beginning, it will be rooting which represents that avenue of discharge which eventually will lead to communication on the semantic level.

Before this can be achieved a large number of successive steps in the development of object relations must be made. The rooting detour of the beginning, of the completely dependent objectless period of the child, led eventually to need gratification, to the gratification of the instinct. A year and a half later the movement pattern of rooting is reactivated in the semantic "No." This time it is endowed with semantic meaning and takes its place as one of the devices used in the object relations which have been developed and consolidated in the meanwhile. These object relations, however, do not originate from rooting. They arise from the direct need gratification achieved by the clinging of the lips and hands.

In the further development of the human being, object relations will always betray their origin, namely consummation of immediate drive gratification. Communication and thought processes, on the other hand, will remain characteristically detour functions, techniques that pave the way to the consummatory act.

When the movement used in the rooting behavior is reactivated in the course of the second year and placed into the service of communication, it will become the semantic sign of "No." Using or not using this sign enables the child to

[66]

determine volitionally the day-to-day vicissitudes of the mother-child relations.

In the intervening eighteen months, cephalogyric motion, originally a *reaction* to tactile stimulation, changes into a volitionally determined *action* expressing a thought process. At the same time this movement, which was a physiologically preformed *behavior* of "striving toward," becomes a gestural *symbol* of "striving away." In this metamorphosis a purely motor pattern becomes invested with semantic significance.

But how does the motor pattern of rooting, which had fallen into disuse for twelve months or more, become available again to the child in his second year for semantic purposes? Can we discern in the semantic gesture of the fifteen-months-old an echo, however faint, of the affect connected with rooting during the first three months of life? We have demonstrated in the previous chapter that identification with the aggressor can be considered as one well-established factor leading to the adoption of the adult's "No" gesture by the child. May we assume that regression to the original rooting movement is a second factor in its use for semantic purposes by the fifteen-months-old? After all, we have seen that regression as a consequence of frustration and unpleasure was operative in the reactivation of rooting in the form of pathologic cephalogyric movements.

Furthermore, regressive facial mimetic behavior going back to nursing has been observed in the adult. An example of this has been reported recently by Adatto in an article on "Pouting" (1956). Pouting is a mimetic movement of the lips observable already in the neonate. In the case described by Adatto, pouting unconsciously had two meanings: it represented a reaching out for the breast, a wish for oral gratification on one hand; on the other it was a reaction to frustration, because it was also a regressive wishful fantasy of a state of satisfactory maternal contact.

Consciously, pouting was a communication of the patient to his social environment; it meant sullenness, and a throttled-down anger, and was understood as such. Like the motor pattern of the semantic head-shaking "No," the motor pattern for pouting originates in the earliest nursing situation and has taken on a meaning very different from the one it possessed originally. *Like the semantic head-shaking "No," pouting has acquired a rather universal semantic meaning transcending national and racial boundaries.*

But we can hardly be surprised to find that early oral behavior is placed into the service of universally accepted semantic signals. Even scientists whose frame of reference disregards psychoanalytic theory like Latif (1934) or Lewis (1936) have stressed that "it is inevitable that any utterance made by the child in connection with feeding should become shaped by the movements of feeding; in discussing the nature of language we cannot evade the fact that the organs of utterance are also the organs of sucking." Spielrein (1922), whose inferences are mostly limited to the straight symbol interpretation extant here and there in the early twenties, holds that in speaking the child reproduces the nursing act with the movements of his mouth and therefore somehow reactivates the sensations experienced during nursing. These authors stress the obvious: namely that the major tool of human semantic communication develops in closest anaclitic connection with orality; that oral experiences provide the very first building blocks for speech; and that without the oral experience of earliest infancy it is very questionable indeed whether man would have speech in the sense in which it is known to us.

This may sound like idle speculation which cannot be

proved or disproved, for how can one circumvent orality in raising a human child? Of course, in the case of bees, where oral contact with another individual of the same species is nonexistent for the purpose of feeding the young, communication takes place in the form of "dances" and not through oral signals. But is it permissible to draw conclusions from such widely different species as man and bee? It is not. We have outlined elsewhere how far, in our opinion, such deductive inferences from one species to another are permissible. Therefore, we will have recourse to the insight which can be obtained from the study of pathological conditions, a method which has so often proved fertile in our science.

9.

By-passing the Cathexis of the Oral Zone

For the purposes of our present study we have traced the origins of rooting behavior along three lines: its phylogenetic precursors in altricials, its embryology in the anencephalic, and its ontogenesis based on our own investigations of the newborn. In all three the functioning of rooting behavior, which is an innate releasing mechanism, was ensured from the beginning through the availability of the releasing stimulus.

In the first part of this monograph we have found that pathological manifestations in emotionally deprived children raised the question of whether rooting behavior has a function for the emergence of communication. We will now expand our ontogenetic approach by tracing the fate of this IRM in circumstances in which the releasing stimulus is unavailable. Specifically, we will explore a case in which the absence of the oral component modified the anaclitic situation in a unique fashion. We will show that this modification of the anaclitic situation resulted in a corresponding modification of the signals of communication, as well as in a change of adaptive and defense behavior.

We have been fortunate in becoming acquainted with a case history that supports our propositions regarding negative cephalogyric movements, negation, and our assumptions of the anaclitic oral origin of semantic communication and speech. Through the courtesy of Drs. George Engel and Franz Reichsman of Rochester, New York, we are permitted to reproduce here the following case history of Monica W.:[1]

Case History

Monica W. was born with esophageal atresia. On the third day of her life an esophageal fistula on the neck, on the fourth day a gastric fistula on the abdomen of the child was established. The baby was nourished through the gastric fistula during the first twenty-one months of her life; at fifteen months she was readmitted to the hospital. At this time she was in a marantic condition. She was treated for this and at the same time a thorough psychiatric and physiologic study, which went on for many months, was made of the child by Drs. Engel and Reichsman. Besides, exact protocols, laboratory examinations of gastric secretions, etc., were made, and an extensive footage of motion pictures (in color) was taken of the "transactions"[2] between Monica and Dr. Reichsman.

[1] The data quoted here are based on mimeographed notes prepared by Drs. Engel and Reichsman for their presentation at the Annual Meeting of the American Psychoanalytic Association, May 1955, as well as on personal communications. The manuscript of the present monograph was already concluded when the first extensive publication on the case by Engel and Reichsman appeared in 1956, too late to include more than this reference to it.

[2] The term "transactions" and "transactional" has been widely used of recent years in psychiatric writings. Originally introduced by Dewey, it is useful in describing processes going on between two or more individuals. In psychoanalytic writing it has the disadvantage of making no difference between processes going on within the subject and processes going on between the subject and others. We will, therefore, continue to use here the term "intrapersonal" for the processes going on within the subject. For the processes going on between the subject and others we will use the term "interpersonal," though we are aware of Kubie's (1953) objections to this term. We share his objections to its misuse; however, if correctly applied, it serves well for descriptive purposes and we have no better term to replace it.

These investigations had been carried on for eight months, when I came to visit Dr. Engel. Dr. Reichsman acted in the role of the "good object," feeding Monica with the help of a funnel through the gastric fistula, while establishing good relations and playing with her. I was permitted to view the motion pictures taken of the child during her stay in the hospital. They showed her behavior during feeding and her relations to various persons. Furthermore, I was permitted to examine Monica personally on June 5, 1954, when she was twenty-three months old.

The child looked a great deal like the deprived children I had observed and described elsewhere. When I approached her, she manifested unmistakable unpleasure. However, she did not produce head-shaking. When I stayed at her bedside, attempting to induce her to make contact with me by turning my back to her (Spitz, 1950), she waved me away with her hand. This is a behavior which I had never observed in deprived children. When she did not succeed in removing my presence through waving her hand, she turned her head away from me, excluding me from her visual perception. I persisted in remaining close to the child's bed, motionless, so that she could reach me if she wished to. After about five minutes, during which she kept her head averted, but from time to time glanced in my direction as if to find out whether I had gone away, she closed her eyes and went to sleep.

Further observation of Monica, as well as a careful perusal of the films taken of her, showed some other peculiarities which distinguished her behavior from that of all other children; these peculiarities were also helpful in interpreting the behavior I have just described.

Some time after my visit another operation was performed on Monica, in which an artificial esophagus connecting the mouth with the stomach was implanted (colonic substernal anastomosis) and the fistula closed, so that the child from then on could be fed by mouth.

To my questions about Monica's preoperative behavior with strangers, Dr. Engel wrote me that, to their and their nursing personnel's best recollection, head-shaking had not been present. After the baby had begun to be fed by mouth, *following the above-described operation,* the nurse stated that head-shaking began to appear as a sign of refusal.[3] Furthermore, in the weeks following the operation head-shaking was observed as a response to hospital personnel who had been associated with experiences disagreeable to the child.

Psychoanalytic Considerations Suggested by the Case Material

The unique features of Monica's case are self-evident. They offer a quasi-experimental validation for Freud's propositions on the oral phase, as well as a striking illustration of the genetic viewpoint. Moreover, the case highlights the role played by the mouth in the ontogenesis of communication— by exclusion, as it were; for in Monica's case the pleasure function of the mouth was divorced from the survival function of nutrition and hence also from object relations.

We have advanced two propositions earlier: (1) that the beginnings of human communication are based on the fact that the mouth is the organ used both for food intake and for speech; (2) that the deprived infant's head-shaking as a sign of refusal is a regression to the behavior patterns connected with nursing by mouth.

In the case of Monica, nursing or regular feeding by mouth had not occurred during the first twenty months of life. During this period feeding took place through the

[3] Letter from Dr. Engel, July 20, 1954.

gastric fistula on the abdomen; and as can be seen in the films, she behaved toward the funnel as a normal child would toward the breast or the bottle, touching it, exploring it, fondling it with her hands during feeding; and pushing it away with her hands when she refused it. She used a similar movement of the hand when she refused my approach.

It would seem that the use of the head for semantic gestures had not been acquired by this two-year-old because oral experience had been divorced from the intake of food, that is from the *anaclitic* situation, *and therefore from object relations*. Accordingly, the behavior patterns this child used in her object relations were of a totally different nature. She refuses contact by turning away from the unwelcome observer, thus excluding him from her visual perception. When this did not lead to results, she used the behavior learned during feeding experience through the abdominal wall: she waved him aside, pushed him away with her hand. This is something which the normal child, whether nursed at the breast or fed with the bottle, does not usually do, because the head, and with it the mouth, can be withdrawn from the nipple; Monica would have had to withdraw the abdominal wall from the funnel. That she cannot do; but she can push the funnel away with her hand—and she tries to do the same with the unwelcome observer. Finally, when these methods were unsuccessful, Monica closed her eyes and withdrew into sleep. We do not know whether in her sleep she possibly may or may not have produced a dream.

It is perhaps useful to point out that at twenty-three months, the age at which I saw her, Monica had not acquired speech in any form. This agrees with our proposition about the decisive role of the oral zone and of anaclitic object relations in achieving human semantic communication. Since in the case of Monica nutrition had been displaced from the mouth to the abdominal fistula, neither the mouth nor the head had been involved specifically in the need-gratificatory relations. Accordingly, she did not even achieve head gestures for the purpose of semantic communication, let alone the use of her mouth for verbalization. It is impressive to find that once feeding through the mouth becomes possible (thanks to the operation of colonic substernal anastomosis), she soon begins to use head-shaking denegation. One may assume that with this the door will also be open for the gradual acquisition of verbal skills.

The Application of Lewin's Propositions to Monica's Case

We have seen that as an ultimate recourse when confronted with an unpleasure stimulus Monica withdraws into sleep. We may ask ourselves how this withdrawal into sleep can be understood in terms of Bertram Lewin's oral triad: to eat, to be eaten, to sleep (to die) (1946). In Lewin's thesis, to go to sleep means to go to sleep at the breast. For Monica the breast is nonexistent. She is only acquainted with tension reduction, which occurs when her stomach is filled through the funnel by Dr. Reichsman.[4] For Monica the perception of the funnel, which goes into the gastric fistula, and the perception of Dr. Reichsman's face, as he administers the food and talks and plays with her, becomes connected with relief from tension through the funnel. When she happens to refuse food, it is still Dr. Reichsman's face which is connected with the situation. In other words, the object relations which she has formed with Dr. Reichsman involve both positive and negative aspects, as is usual.

The following hypothesis then appears permissible: The establishment of Dr. Reichsman's face as the representative

4 See also Tilney and Casamajor (1924), on the specific effect that the filling of the stomach has on the newborn's behavior pattern.

[75]

of the object, good and bad, leads to Monica's turning away her head from me, the unwelcome stranger. When this proves ineffective, she closes her eyes and excludes all visual perception. When even these methods are insufficient to abolish the unwelcome intrusion, Monica goes one step further in her withdrawal and goes to sleep. We believe that this is a regression to the archaic sleep of satiation after having been fed.

We may then speak of sleep as the prototype of all defense. In the sense of Freud's *Three Essays on the Theory of Sexuality,* we may call it an *anaclitic defense,* for it leans onto the physiological function of sleep. In the neonate, sleep is a normal protective function which falls under the wider concept of the stimulus barrier. It is the withdrawal of cathexis from the sensorium. The uncathected sensorium acts as the most effective barrier against unwelcome afferent stimuli.

By falling asleep for the purpose of avoiding a stranger Monica places an otherwise normal behavior into the service of defense. It is a successful avoidance of unpleasure by means of a regression; pathological negative cephalogyric movements in deprived children are an attempt with the same purpose, though an unsuccessful one. Actually, the deprived infants have stopped halfway on the road. Monica's regression is a deeper one, she has gone the whole way to quiescence.

Regression as a defense against unpleasure stimuli employs a withdrawal to a level in the subject's psychic organization on which that particular stimulus did not or could not cause unpleasure and on which freedom from unpleasure was equivalent to pleasure. This is what we do daily in going to sleep, in the course of which a temporal and a topograpical regression takes place (Freud, 1924). Going to sleep is the device used by Monica. With Lewin, we may assume that going to sleep at the breast is equivalent to satiation, that is the absence of the unpleasure of hunger. This interpretation holds also for Monica. Only in her case it is not going to sleep at the breast, but going to sleep "with a filled stomach" which corresponds to the absence of unpleasure stimuli. Regression enables her to achieve the hallucinatory gratification of a filled stomach. This is a coenesthetic experience; not the external, tactile and visual one of which Lewin speaks. In going to sleep, Monica successfully replaces the perceptual unpleasure experience of the stranger's unwelcome face with the hallucinated pleasure of satiation.

Lewin's theory (1946, 1950) invites some further speculations along the lines of the ideas expressed above. In his assumption the visual percept of the breast is the origin of the dream screen; I expanded this assumption and suggested that the oral experience mediated by the primal cavity (Spitz, 1955a) antedates the visual percept of the breast. Both these propositions imply learning, the accumulation of experiences, be they visual in the case of Lewin's assumptions, be they tactile in those voiced by me. The findings in the case of Monica suggest that even earlier than the tactile perceptions of the mouth, and more fundamental because unlearned, the relief from unpleasure tension may have functioned as the most archaic matrix for the dream screen.

The sequence which leads to the phenomenon of the dream screen in the adult would then be the following: the experience of tension reduction on the coenesthetic level, followed by the experience of the cavity sensation on the level of nondifferentiation, and culminating in the percept of the breast on the level of diacritic visual perception. Therefore, the dream screen of the adult appears to be a representation of the most archaic human pleasure experience. It uses for this representation the archaic materials still available to the

[77]

adult, i.e., coenesthetic sensations, and the later transition from these to the perception of visual images in the dream screen. The use of this archaic pre-imagery material is imposed through the necessity of representing an experience from the level of the Nirvana principle, namely, tension reduction.

The dream screen in its earliest origin is an inchoate experience of variations in tensions; when it becomes conscious in the adult's dream, it has already passed through several levels of nascent psychic development. It is an attempt at representation with the help of the specific psychic material that is characteristic for each of these levels. Its ultimate appearance as a screen is the result of the functioning of the secondary process. Regard for representability is one of the tasks of the secondary process. It will, therefore, supply from the memory images available to the adult those which come closest both chronologically and in terms of experience (that is, feeling tone) to the original experience of tension reduction. From the point of view of visual perception, that is the picture of the breast.

However, the dream screen is not perceived visually in every dream. In the Isakower phenomenon the percept is more tactile than visual. Finally, as implied by Lewin in his paper on "The Forgetting of Dreams" (1953), "pure emotion" may be the form in which the dream screen is experienced without the representations of a secondary elaboration in terms of sensory images.

If that is the case, then it becomes evident that in one of these three forms the dream screen is demonstrable in every dream. For in every dream at least a feeling tone is experienced, be it that of happiness, of sadness, of dreary indifference or of panic. The feeling tone in our dreams would be the way in which the adult is able to describe the experiences

[78]

of tension reduction and the degrees of increase of tension. Indeed, the extraordinary vividness which these feeling tones can assume in the dream makes it highly probable that they originate in a period in which they represented the alpha and omega of all experience.

Lewin's original proposition defines the dream screen as that component of the dream onto which the dreamer projects his images. This becomes readily understandable as a result of what we have just suggested. Crudely expressed, a dream would then come about as follows: day residues of the nature of what I like to call "unfinished business," that is, waking experiences which are unresolved and leave tension behind, disturb the sleeper's slumber. There the feeling tone of these tensions finds its resonance at the level of the deepest regression, at that of the Nirvana principle. A degree of tension striving toward reduction is established in a first step. Regard for representability calls forth with the help of the secondary process the primitive image of the breast, that is, the dream screen.

However, the perceptual elements of the day residue have accompanied the tensions in their retrogression through the Mem systems and have activated kindred or associated memory traces. In the progressive process toward system Pcpt, the secondary process combines these elements into a more or less plausible story which takes place against the background of the dream screen. This step represents the effort toward tension reduction. The vagaries of the story are governed by the more or less successful attempts at discharging tension. Their success is predicated on the measure of ego (superego) syntonicity of the successive attempts at discharge. Whether the paradigmatic dream published by Lewin, in which the dream screen rolls up on itself, rolls away and carries the dream with it, represents a successful discharge

[79]

of the dreamer's tension or a repression of the dream, is beyond this author's capacity to decide.

Another question is whether one should assume that the third element in Lewin's oral triad, namely death, is represented in Monica's withdrawal into sleep. Her withdrawal annihilates the unwelcome intruder by excluding him first from her visual perception and then from her consciousness. Shall we assume that this exclusion is a projection onto the intruder of Monica's wish to eat, to be eaten, to die? Death certainly is the constant companion of this child, and one might speculate whether with the help of this projection Monica, in falling asleep, becomes able to gratify simultaneously the libidinal drive through the hallucinatory fantasy of satiation, and the aggressive drive through the annihilation of the intruder?

The Experience of Gratification and Regression

There is a fundamental difference between the device used by Monica to achieve tension reduction (withdrawing into sleep) and the attempt at withdrawal of cephalogyric children. Monica, having had no oral food intake experience, had to regress to the straightforward gratification of the drive, to the equivalent of a full stomach, that is, to sleep. The deprived children did have gratifying oral experiences up to three months of age, when the precursor of the object is formed. Therefore, their oral experiences were established in the framework of the precursors of object relations, namely of nursing at the breast. They halted their regression at the behavior leading to what we have called the *matrix of object relations,* namely, oral intake at the breast.

This difference in the level to which Monica regressed versus the level to which the deprived children regress illuminates the experiential significance of object relationships.

[80]

Already at such an early age, the experience of the relation to the object—even though at this stage it is only the need-satisfying rather than the love object—takes on an extraordinary emotional valency. In the case of the deprived children this experience had become a fixation point to which they could regress. They regressed to the exact event which preceded the happy gratification of the need. It is also the behavior which marked that their need had *not yet* been gratified. Monica, on the contrary, could only regress to the most archaic, to the coenesthetic functional experience.

Another interesting aspect of this speculation is that the second member of the oral triad, namely, to be eaten, appears nowhere in Monica's behavior; and, indeed, how should it? That presupposes the experience of the cavity sensation in the mouth, concomitant with the enveloping arms (Spitz, 1955a). The combination of these two never existed in Monica's world. The experience which did exist was that of tension reduction through satiation.

The Ethological Implications of Monica's Case

In discussing the ethological implications which the case of Monica suggests, we will refer our readers to our remarks on the innate releasing mechanism (IRM) on page 30n. The case of Monica provides an important contribution to the ethological propositions on the innate releasing mechanism in man. As a result of a pathological condition, in the case of Monica a specific preformed *phylogenetic* pattern, rooting behavior, did not materialize. It was replaced by an *onto-genetically* developed behavior which she improvised in response to the particular circumstances of her nutrition.

Phylogenetically, rooting is unquestionably one of the most firmly established behavior patterns. However, the case of Monica demonstrates that even this phylogenetically

[81]

firmly established inherited pattern only becomes effective when the releaser stimulus, namely the stimulation of the snout, is forthcoming, and that the pattern will not respond to all and any stimuli. In other terms, we are dealing with the complementary parts of a total phenomenon. To every innate releasing mechanism belongs a releaser stimulus. It may, as was the case with Monica, *lie in abeyance* for two years. When finally the releaser stimulus was provided, when as a result of the surgically established mouth-stomach connection Monica takes food through the mouth, the missing element is introduced into the original pattern of the innate releasing mechanism. When, with the help of the last operation, this missing factor was introduced into the framework of the object relations which Monica had already established, the archaic rooting pattern was triggered and activated; and cephalogyric movements could become meaningful. Thereupon head-shaking, endowed with the meaning of refusal, was used by the child in her object relations.

A more extensive discussion of the principles of the innate releasing mechanism, of behavior patterns and their underlying components would lead us too far from our main subject; but we want to go on record with the opinion that it is not only the rooting pattern which will remain in abeyance if the releaser stimulus is not forthcoming. We believe that the same may apply to many other phylogenetically preformed patterns, and probably even to the laws of maturation. I believe that animal ethologists would not reject this proposition. I presume that they might qualify it, limiting the span of time during which a phylogenetic behavior pattern can lie in abeyance, by what has been called by Scott and Marston (1950) "critical stages." As a psychoanalyst I feel inclined to agree; I have postulated the existence of such developmental stages on the grounds of my observations and spoken of them as "organizers of psychological development" (Spitz, 1954). We will discuss this concept in greater detail in Chapter XII.

We have then two propositions: (1) that phylogenetically preformed, inherited behavior patterns can lie in abeyance until such time as the releaser stimulus becomes available; (2) that the span of time is limited to the critical period marked by the emergence of the "organizer." The two propositions are interdependent in regard to further development; for development will take a deviant course when a phylogenetically preformed and developmentally important behavior pattern is inhibited. Monica probably is an example in point. If this proposition can be substantiated by further observations it would have far-reaching implications for our assumptions on the formation of some of the forms of fixation, and consequently might also offer certain suggestions in the field of psychiatric therapy.

Summary

The Engel-Reichsman case is a welcome confirmation of my assumptions regarding the origin and the significance of the negative cephalogyric movements of children suffering from hospitalism, a confirmation, so to say, *e contrario*. But, more important, it contributes additional observational data to the psychoanalytic theory of the libidinal phases and the erotogenic zones. Furthermore, it provides an impressive illustration of the object choice according to the anaclitic mode. The anaclitic choice of object is determined by the original dependence of the infant on the person who feeds, protects and mothers him. Freud states that in the beginning the drive unfolds anaclitically, that is by leaning onto a need gratification essential for survival. The need which is gratified is the need for food. Accordingly, the first erotogenic zone is the oral zone and the whole period was called the oral phase.

In the case of Monica, the oral zone was precluded from functioning. Thereupon, the drive quite manifestly (as demonstrated in the motion picture) leaned onto the function of what I will tentatively call *para-oral* food intake; an erotization of the gastric fistula took place (Margolin, 1953). Furthermore, a libidinization of the function of being nourished through the funnel is observable; the child treats the funnel as the origin of food; she forms her object relation to the giver of food and care, Dr. Reichsman. Accordingly, for Monica, Dr. Reichsman became the "good object." But also, intermittently, he became the "bad object," as is the case in the early stages of the formation of all object relations in general. This found its expression in Monica's characteristic reaction to the occasional ups and downs of Dr. Reichsman's emotional climate; when Dr. Reichsman was absent because of some outside event, Monica showed in the subsequent feeding situation that she resented his desertion. All this is beautifully demonstrated by her behavior in the motion pictures, and at the same time by the change in the composition of her gastric secretions, chemical analysis of which was made concurrently.

On the other hand, everybody who was not connected with the feeding and protecting situation was a stranger, and she reacted to him accordingly. I was such a stranger and she refused contact with me. But she did not refuse by producing a reaction similar to that of a child raised in the oral-anaclitic situation. She *created* a new set of behavior patterns, including *signals* which were not in reference to the oral pattern of nourishment, of oral intake, but were in reference to the gastric fistula pattern of nutrition.

Monica developed her individual and original set of

signals in terms of her particular feeding situation. This supports our proposition that the techniques and the modes of communication are developed from the anaclitic situation, normally from the infant's earliest relation with the breast. Under normal circumstances the phylogenetically preformed pattern of the rooting behavior becomes the matrix of the semantic gesture of negative head-shaking. We have already stressed that the acquisition of this gesture is a momentous intellectual achievement, connected with the function of judgment (Chapter VII).

The extraordinary consistency in the linkage between the beginnings of semantic communication and thought processes on one hand, earliest mother-child relations on the other, will be a warning to the thoughtful. We may well wonder how extensively feeding babies a formula from a propped bottle may have influenced the development of Western mind in the last fifty to eighty years. That such an influence can be demonstrated in individual development is a matter of record. But the more important question arises of how this may have influenced changes in the ways of Western man, in the ways of his communication, and whether and how it has influenced his relations to his environment, his verbal and nonverbal symbols, and perhaps also his thinking processes.

10.

Theoretical Considerations

We can now proceed in an attempt to integrate our understanding of the head-shaking "No" in theoretical terms with the help of the insight we have gained in the preceding chapter. We will be guided by the line of thought provided by Freud (1895a, p. 379), when he stated: "This path of discharge thus acquires an extremely important secondary function—viz., of bringing about an understanding [or rather: communication] with other people." Thirty years later Freud elaborated some of the implications of this brief statement in his article on "Negation" (1925). The far-reaching significance of this essay has been discussed most recently by Rapaport (1951).

The number of major problems on which Freud sheds light in these five brief pages is extraordinary. To mention only a few, he discusses the nature of perception, that of reality testing and some of the principles of intellectual function. He explores the function of judgment, its origin from, and relation to, the primary drives and establishes it as that function of the intellect which substitutes for repression. If we interpret him correctly, he outlines the role of the "symbol of negation" in communication, where it makes feasible the achievement of the function of judgment by endowing thought "with a first degree of independence from the result of repression and at the same time from the sway of the pleasure principle."

Freud speaks specifically of the "*symbol*[1] of negation." Here the term *symbol* has a different meaning from the one he uses in the discussion of dreams, folklore, mythology or poetry. In these "the symbolic relation is essentially that of a comparison" (Freud, 1917, p. 136). The symbol in this sense is a representation (be this true representation, substitution or allusion). As such it lends itself both to the mental processes going on *within* the individual and to communications going on *between* individuals.

Negation, and its expression, the word "No," is different from such symbols. The word "No" implies no comparison with an existing representation. It is what logicians call an algorithmic symbol, just like the minus sign in mathematics. Algorithmic symbols, such as the "symbol of negation," are specifically reserved for interindividual communication. We will conclude therefore that in this article, Freud, while discussing negation from the viewpoints of the thought process, of the drives and of repression, had in mind also the role of the symbol of negation for the purposes of communication.

Judgment and communication are the two subjects which will occupy us in the present chapter. In the article on "Negation" Freud discusses these problems in terms of conscious and unconscious in the descriptive sense; in terms of the instincts and drives; and furthermore in the terms of the ego, that is, of the structural model.[2]

This is the frame of reference which Freud had elaborated

1 Italics mine.
2 It might be questioned whether Freud was really applying the structural model in this paper, as in examining the function of judgment he only speaks of the ego. However, at the inception of judgment in the infant, the ego and the id are the only two components of the structural model which have been differentiated out of the nondifferentiated phase.

by 1925, when he wrote "Negation." In 1895, in the "Project for a Scientific Psychology," where he wrote on the path of discharge of excitation and its function in bringing about communication (quoted above), his emphasis was on object relations within the dyad. While in 1895 Freud was discussing psychology in terms of the relations of the individual with his environment, in 1925 he was studying the problem of negation primarily in terms of endopsychic processes. We will now endeavor to integrate Freud's earlier and later approach, that of object relations with that of the structural and dynamic viewpoint.

Achieving the faculty of judgment is a decisive step in the development of the thinking process, both from the viewpoint of the child's psychic economy and from that of psychic structure. A negative judgment is the intellectual substitute for repression.[3] It is more efficient than repression in several ways. On one hand, it represents a saving in psychic energy, on the other it is more effective in achieving the goal of the drive. Furthermore, it represents an extraordinary reinforcement of the structure of the ego, of which it is, and increasingly will become, one of the major functions. These are the reasons why substituting the intellectual operation of judg-

[3] Freud's formulation of negation as a substitute for repression has undergone certain qualifications in present-day psychoanalytic thinking. The repression of which Freud speaks is a very archaic phenomenon in the infant's life. It corresponds more to the withdrawal of cathexis from a percept and not to the defense mechanism of repression with which we are familiar after psychic structure has been fully developed. Obviously, repression as a defense mechanism also involves a withdrawal of cathexis; but there is more to repression.

We would be inclined to distinguish three stages in the development of repression: (1) primal repression (*Urverdrängung*); (2) repression proper (*Nachdrängen*), which consists of two phases; namely (a) the early precursor of repression (or "primitive repression"), consisting of withdrawal of cathexis; (b) repression as a defense mechanism which involves countercathexis. The negative judgment would substitute for phase (a) of repression proper, namely the withdrawal of cathexis.

ment for repression is such an important advance.

The function of judgment is concerned ultimately with two sorts of decisions. It may assert or deny that a thing has a particular property; or it may assert or dispute that a particular image exists in reality (Freud, 1925).

Rooting—A Prestage of Communication

However, at the beginning of life, no judgment, be it negative or positive, is available, at least in the form of observable behavior. The decision whether a thing has or has not a particular property, the assertion or the denial that a particular image exists, is meaningless at this stage. None of these categories applies to the rooting behavior; it signifies the wish to take the nipple in; but even this statement is misleading, it is not a wish, for in the first weeks of life volition is nonexistent. Stated correctly, we will say that "taking the nipple in" is the consummation of the approach *function* of rooting.

Rooting is unique among the activities of the newborn in several respects. All other activities at birth are uncoordinated, random, and show no reliable or predictable pattern. Even responses and reflexes are unreliable. In fact, behavior in the sense of an organized pattern of activity is nonexistent in the begining, with one single exception: that is the rooting behavior. Rooting shows a relatively high degree of coordination, it is directed, it is goal-specific and success-specific, for the behavior goes on until the goal is reached and stops when the goal is achieved. It is the one behavior pattern in which the drive is visibly manifested and which shows a gradient to need reduction. The positive "striving toward" quality of the drive finds expression in the directedness of rooting.

It is significant that rooting has no negative counterpart;

in the newborn's activity no "striving away" corresponds to the "striving toward." No behavior expressing a negative and showing any directedness or organized pattern exists in the neonate. That which might pass for a negative takes the form of random, disorganized, diffuse unpleasure manifestations.

This nonexistence of an organized expression of the negative in the neonate is the observational duplicate of Freud's postulate: ". . . we never discover a 'No' in the unconscious . . ." (1925). And, of course, consciousness, or even perception cannot be demonstrated in the newborn, nor can volition. When perception, memory, consciousness and volition emerge somewhere in the course of the third month of life, the infant's behavior can begin to express refusal; until then refusal takes a physiological form at best; namely, the child stops sucking or vomits what it has ingested.

The dichotomies established by Freud in his article on "Negation," the alternative in the judgment of asserting or denying that a thing has a particular property, can be expressed in the language of the oral instinctual impulses; as Freud puts it: "I should like to eat that, or I should like to spit it out." Or, carrying it one stage further: "It is to be either inside me, or outside me." It seems to me that at birth the alternative could be formulated according to the Nirvana principle in the following terms: "This is tension reducing; that is tension creating." What is tension reducing is taken in. What is tension creating is ejected, the baby spits it out.

However, already at birth there is a third modality which is neither taking in nor spitting out. It is activated by tension originating *inside* of the infant, specifically tension connected with the need for food intake. The modalities of taking in and spitting out are determined by an innate preformed pattern.

"Taking in" and "spitting out" are consummatory behaviors. They cannot be immediately implemented when the hunger tension arises. They have to be, and are, preceded by a scanning and searching behavior, with the quality of "striving toward" to make the "taking in," the consummation possible (Fenichel, 1945, p. 83).[4]

It is of great theoretical interest that rooting, the matrix of the semantic function, is a behavior which is neither spitting out nor taking in, but which is a *scanning* behavior, provoked by a state of tension, that is, by instinctual drives which seek gratification. Freud's far-reaching concept links the path of excitation discharge at birth with the evolution of human communication which emerges in the second year of life. We have now filled in some of the details of this evolution through our finding that the matrix of semantic function is a scanning behavior provoked by need tension.

Moreover, the finding that communication and semantic function originate from scanning behavior supplements in a meaningful way similar postulates set forth by Freud on the nature of perception and on that of the thought process. He remarked in his paper on "Negation" that "the ego periodically sends out small amounts of cathectic energy into the perceptual system and by their means *samples* the external stimuli, and after every such groping advance draws back again."[5] In regard to the thought process, Freud (1911) states that it is an experimental way of acting, accompanied by displacement of small quantities of cathexis (along memory traces).

---

[4] We have established previously that rooting is a phylogenetic behavior pattern. Our present argument shows it to be also an adaptive pattern. For it is a detour function to achieve the aim of the drive, which is food intake. As such it might be considered a prototype for the reality principle and should fall into the category of ego nuclei (Glover, 1933, 1935, 1943).

[5] Italics mine. See also Freud (1925, p. 180; 1920, pp. 24-28; 1900, p. 538; and 1895a, p. 359 pass.).

[91]

The genesis of communication from scanning, of course, assigns it a role in the function of reality testing. This role remains very much in evidence in specific forms of adult verbal communication, such as questions, question sentences, and, on the highest level, discussion. The genesis of communication, furthermore, has in common with reality testing that they both originate from a need. We have shown this to be so in the case of rooting; of reality testing Freud stated that its essential precondition is that objects shall have been lost which formerly afforded real satisfaction.

We mentioned earlier that Freud described perception as well as thought processes in terms of what today we would call a scanning activity of the psychic apparatus. In the case of perception he specifically spoke of "sampling," in the case of the thought process he spoke of a "trial action." We may add to this that this scanning activity takes place according to the model of the so-called "trial-and-error" behavior of all animals. This behavior was extensively studied in the paramecium and can be observed also in the mammals. In the newborn human child it appears in the form of rooting. It consists in an action which samples the surround, withdraws, repeats the sampling in another direction, etc., until the goal of need gratification is achieved. Perception does the same with a lesser expenditure of muscular energy. Thought process, finally, is a scanning of the inner representation of the surround, without any expenditure of muscular energy and with minimal quanta of cathexis.

Up to this point our considerations have enabled us to situate the pattern of rooting at a stage at which even the vaguest beginnings of the development of judgment or of intentional communication are still in the very distant future. We have not yet been able to find a satisfactory connection between rooting as the matrix of communication and the eventual emergence of the semantic gesture of head-shaking "No." The pathological cephalogyric motions of deprived children were of no help in this endeavor, because they turned out to have a regressive significance, linking them with rooting behavior, and not a progressive one in the direction of the semantic signal.

Avoidance—An Intermediate Stage

We therefore returned once more to our observations of the nursing child and reviewed the later evolution of his behavior patterns. As already stated, the rooting pattern becomes gradually goal-adapted through the elimination of unnecessary excursions of the head. Increasing coordination of tactile perception and muscle action, as well as of visual perception after the third month, collaborate in making the intake of the nipple into the mouth ever swifter and surer, until one sweep of the head secures it. At this stage rooting has practically disappeared.

Simultaneously with this process and independently from it, the child develops a new behavior with which he indicates his satiation and his wish to end the meal. He turns his head from side to side energetically, away from the pursuing nipple. This is quite different from his passive behavior in the first half year, during which the satiated child, lips flaccidly relaxed, abandons the nipple, and falls asleep at the breast. A further introduction of the nipple elicits no response. But a few months later, when muscle coordination begins to function and the first elements of a central steering organization are established, the satiated child will signify his refusal of further food by eluding the nipple actively.

This avoidance behavior is quite similar in its motor aspects to rooting movements. But while the pattern of the movement has not changed, its purpose has become the opposite. Rooting had the function of finding the nipple; the avoidance behavior signifies refusal of the nipple. The very same movement, when it reappears in the second year of life as the "No" gesture, is endowed with the meaning of the avoidance behavior (namely refusal).

I believe that we may postulate that the avoidance gesture of the satiated three- to six-months-old provides the missing link between rooting movements and the eventual use of the same motor pattern in the "No" gesture. The genetic sequence which leads to the head-shaking "No" thus has proved to consist of three stages: (1) rooting, a phylogenetically established motor pattern of scanning, appearing on the level of nondifferentiation; (2) satiated avoidance behavior, a conscious refusal, appearing at the inception of elementary reciprocal object relations; (3) head-shaking "No," a semantic gesture, at the level of object relations at which semantic communication with the help of verbal symbols is initiated by the acquisition of the symbol of negation.

Each of the first two phases contributes to the third. While rooting provides the motor matrix, satiated avoidance behavior provides the affective and intellectual category of refusal, with which the movement is ultimately endowed.

The refusal through head-rotating avoidance emerges at the stage at which the earliest ego organization has just come into being. This form of volitional refusal behavior in the feeding situation continues during the progressive unfolding of the ego in the months which follow. It is carried over into the cup-feeding stage, leaving numberless conscious memory traces of the movement's effectiveness. This process of accretion ensures a plausible continuity of the refusal signification of the head-shaking movement.

Another aspect of the first two phases is that while in rooting lateral rotation of the head *initiates* the nursing of the newborn, the movement undergoes a change of function three months later and is used to *terminate* nursing, as an avoidance and refusal behavior.

Since Freud's discussion (1910) on a linguistic study of Abel we take it as a matter of course that primal words have two meanings, one of which is the exact opposite of the other. It could be expected that the same would apply to primal gestures, which actually in the case of the "No" are the precursors of words. In the case of primal words the antithetic sense is present simultaneously. In rooting and in its ulterior developments the antithetic sense is not there from the beginning.

At birth, rooting has the function of approach toward need gratification. As such it expresses seeking, desiring, accepting. The nipple avoidance behavior between three and six months expresses the opposite, namely refusal. As we shall presently see, this refusal quality of the movement becomes the permanent one. The same movement will continue to express refusal during the vicissitudes of cup-feeding and ultimately, after fifteen months of life, will be used as the "No" gesture.

Primal Words

One may then speculate whether there are other primal words in the case of which the antithetical meanings were separate at the origin, then joined into the antithetical word itself and then again separated through usage. We have no material to substantiate this speculation.

It could be objected that the word which develops from the "No" gesture is the epitome, a word which has a univocal meaning and not an antithetical one. To that we must reply that, as can be seen from the example mentioned in Chapter VII, p. 55, there is a period in the second year in which the child, when offered something, will loudly say "No," shaking his head; and at the same time reach for the offered object. It remains to be investigated whether in this particular phenomenon there does not ensue a cleavage between two parts of the child's ego. One part, the one which is in opposition to the grownup, uses the "No" in identification with the aggressor. The other part, intent on his own desires, reaches out for the desired object.

It would of course be simpler to explain this phenomenon as an instance of infantile ambivalence. We feel, however, that the problem of infantile ambivalence requires further clarification. Ambivalence is particularly impressive during the whole first year of life. Consequently, the problems it raises are intimately linked with the phenomenon of non-differentiation. A detailed discussion of all its facets would lead us too far afield; we will therefore limit ourselves to stating that in our opinion the differentiation of "Yes" and "No" is one of its facets. The above-described discrepancy between the child's word and his action would indicate, in our belief, that at this point the child's ego has not yet been completely integrated.[6]

The Meaning of Rooting for the Mother

For the purpose of establishing a beginning of communication between mother and child even as gross a difference as that between "Yes" and "No" is immaterial. What the mother perceives in rooting is a specific motor behavior of the child which she can interpret, and which therefore functions as a signal. This motor behavior remains the same whether the child strives toward the nipple or refuses it. For the mother, this motor behavior, this signal, is an indi-

---

[6] Bychowski (1956) described a regression to such unintegrated ego stages in pathological conditions.

cator of the child's need. She decides with the help of the situational sequence whether the child's need is to receive the nipple or to get rid of it. There is no reason to believe that the ambiguity of the signal which the mother perceives in the child will impair its effectiveness in establishing the beginnings of a communication system between the two.

We propose that the successive appearance of rooting behavior, then refusal of the nipple, and finally the semantic "No" gesture in the course of development is a genetic sequence. This proposition provides us with a plausible account of the developmental vicissitudes of the inborn motor behavior pattern of rooting, up to the point where its motor element becomes incorporated into a semantic gesture. Our other proposition, namely that the global (though by no means universal) usage of the semantic "No" gesture does not rest only on the toddler's identificatory processes but also on a genetic predisposition to the gesture itself, is now substantially documented and can stand on its own merits.

A Speculation on Prehistory

We may therefore, without prejudicing the above argument and independently from it, be permitted to indulge in a speculation regarding the role of certain features of child nursing in man's prehistory and its possible influence on the development of communication.

It is a well-known ethnological fact that in so-called "primitive" societies (probably better designated as preliterate societies) nursing is not limited to the first year of life, but continues right through the toddler age and sometimes up to the third and fourth year (Ploss-Bartels, 1927), when it becomes desultory and ceases gradually. Therefore, in these societies, at an age at which the child's ego is already well established, nursing behavior still forms an integral part of

[97]

the mother-child relation and participates in the emergence of semantic gesture. The various behavior patterns of nursing will thus become available for the purposes of communication *through a process of change of function*.[7] Consequently, nipple-refusing behavior is continued in an unbroken line beyond the level of signal to that of symbol formation.

Reciprocal Identification

We may add to this speculation another well-known fact; i.e., that parents the world over have the tendency to imitate their children's gestures and words—playfully, or for the purpose of communicating with them. There is hardly a family in which some words from the child's vocabulary are not incorporated into the "little language," into the private dialect of the family. It is not always realized that it is not only the children who imitate the parents, but also the parents who imitate the children.

We spoke of this tendency earlier in discussing identification (Chapter VII, pp. 41-42) and showed that the playful mutual imitation of gesture and word is rewarding both for the adult and for the child. We will add here that nearly without exception the infantile terms and gestures incorporated into the "little language" carry the implication of a humorous allusion, of a joke. They are the evidence of an understanding between the persons using them, a secret from which the rest of the world is excluded. In their quality of joke these terms function as releasers for unconscious tensions in the adult, inasmuch as they invite guilt-free regression to uncon-

[7] The motor pattern of head rotation in rooting is a searching technique with the function of *approach,* which in our conceptual framework has an affirmative quality. Head rotation undergoes a change of function when, after three months of development, it is used as a nipple-refusing behavior. The function of affirmative approach is changed into the function of refusal (negative withdrawal). The negative quality makes head rotation suitable to be the motor prototype of the semantic "No" gesture.

scious infantile contents. Playful mutual imitation with its conscious and unconscious rewards appears therefore a likely vehicle of mankind for the transmission of the infantile gesture to the world.

We wonder whether it would be overstretching the license accorded to speculation to consider the possibility that the child's nipple-refusing behavior has been and still is playfully imitated the world over by the mothers. In this act they would be taking over one of the hypothetical meanings of the "No" gesture. This is the meaning derived from the nipple-refusing avoidance behavior, which refers to the plenty and means "No" in the sense of *not* wanting what *is* there. In the terms of Freud: "It is to be . . . outside me."

The other meaning of the "No" gesture is that of something not *being* there, of not finding something. In the terms of Freud, it is a judgment as to the existence of something. This meaning is derived from the function of the rooting behavior's motor pattern, namely, scanning the environment and discovering the nipple.

"No" as Abstraction

The volitional use of the ideational content of negation in the semantic "No" gesture is beyond doubt the most spectacular intellectual and semantic achievement in early childhood. It plays a large role in the child's relations with his environment. And, more important, it is the manifest signal of the child's exercise of the function of judgment. It is probably the first conquest of the gestural or verbal symbol of an abstract concept.

Words to designate concrete things and persons are partly acquired, partly created much earlier by children. They appear already at the end of the first year in the form of "global words" like *Ma-ma*. The first global word is used by the child

[99]

to communicate his needs to the libidinal object, that is to the mother, who is also his executive. It signifies indiscriminately hunger, boredom, discomfort, etc., and the wish to be relieved of them, just as it signifies biscuit, toy, mother and the desire for these. Other such global words are acquired in the following weeks by the child and a certain measure of specialization of single words is achieved. These first verbal symbols signifying needs manifestly are, to use Karl Buehler's classification, still in the nature of an appeal and not of a description.

A new level of integration is achieved after eighteen months of life. The verbal symbols which are now acquired are used not only for the purpose of appeal, but also for the purpose of description, and a specific individual syntax is elaborated. We need not go into the details of this development beyond stating that now the verbal symbols can fulfill the function of abstraction. In the terms of Kubie (1953), the child has acquired the symbolic function.

I believe that the gesture of *semantic* negative head-shaking is the visible indicator of the fact that the abstraction of a refusal or a denial has been achieved by the child. This is the first such abstraction and its symbolic gesture represents the abstract concept of the attitude: "I do not want this." As such it is the first step on the road to the much vaster symbolic function in the verbal field which begins in the second half of the second year. The importance which the achievement of this single particular abstraction, the head-shaking "No," represents for the child is manifested in the fact that it becomes, so to say, the triumphant slogan of a whole period in the child's development of which psychoanalysts had variously spoken as the child's negativistic period. Both Freud (1908) and Anna Freud (1951) have spoken of this period also as that of anal stubbornness.

[100]

The concept of "No" does not exist in the unconscious. The negative is a creation of the ego and is placed into the service of the ego's judgment function. Its eventual emergence is predicated, therefore, on the establishment of the ego's earliest functions, namely on conscious discrimination, and on the inception of the secondary process. From this beginning, a process of evolution, going on throughout the entire first year, leads to the formation of what we may call the ideational concept of the negative. This is achieved in the second year, between the fifteenth and eighteenth month of life. At this point the motor pattern (rooting) is reactivated and the head-shaking "No" gesture becomes the manifest expression of the negative.

This consideration makes it advisable to review once more the two aspects in the origin, in the development and in the emergence of the semantic "No" gesture. One is the ideational content, the other is the motor pattern.

The first of the two, the ideational concept of the negative, has its precursor in the nursing situation at three months. Specifically, in the third month of life the child becomes able to refuse the nipple volitionally. He becomes able to signify a decision through head rotation. It is noteworthy that this achievement coincides with the appearance of the smiling response. We believe that on the road to the eventual consolidation of the negative in the second year, the eight-months anxiety will be one of the stations. We shall discuss our reasons for this belief in Chapter XII. For the present we will point out the change which has taken place from the forerunners of negation in the third month to the consolidation of its varied ideational contents in the second year. The dichotomy in the third month consists in the statement: "I should like to take this into me and keep that out of me." After the consolidation of the concept of the negative this dichotomy is transposed into an abstract judgment which asserts or denies that a thing has a particular property. This was in essence also the decision made in wishing to take something in or to keep something out, for this decision will evolve into the judgment of: "This is good and that is bad."

The second aspect, the motor pattern of the "No" gesture, goes back to birth. Its prototype is rooting, a behavior preformed in phylogenesis. Rooting involves no decision and lacks ideational content.

Both the ideational content of the gesture and its motor pattern are derived from the early stages of the nursing situation. But while the continuity of the conceptual content is evident, the motor pattern undergoes a change of function in the third month. While rooting at the origin involved no decision, the same motor pattern takes over in the third month the function of refusal of the nipple. The continued use of this phylogenetically transmitted motor pattern in the "No" gesture appears like an archaic remnant from the anaclitic situation—to quote Freud: "a certificate of origin, as it were, like 'made in Germany' " (1925).

11.

Affirmation and Its Motor Prototype

Bᴜᴛ when all is said and done, we realize that we have spoken only of "No." Just as familiar as the "No" gesture is the head-nodding "Yes" which signifies assent and affirmation. It is just as widely disseminated on the globe as the head-shaking "No." Our investigation shows that the wide dissemination of the head-shaking "No" is the consequence of the genetic derivation of this gesture from a universal experience of mankind, namely from the nursing situation. The ubiquity of the head-nodding "Yes" encourages us to investigate whether it also has an archaic motor prototype in the nursing situation.

In the case of the head-shaking "No" we discovered that its emergence around the fifteenth month of life was the ultimate result of the confluence of two independent lines of development, namely: (a) an ideational content, ontogenetically developed from an oral instinctual behavior and then put through a metapsychological processing; (b) the vicissitudes of a phylogenetically inherited motor pattern, rooting. We propose to explore the genesis of the "Yes" gesture along the same lines.

Let us recall our findings on the ideational content of the

[103]

"No" gesture and negation. At birth and during the period in which the rooting pattern operates, "No" is nonexistent. The apparatus necessary to perform a judgment is absent, because consciousness does not exist and the unconscious is incapable of negation.

The absence of consciousness in the neonate would seem to show that assent, or, as we prefer to call it, "affirmation," also does not exist at birth. But this is not quite correct in terms of psychoanalytic thinking. It is correct as regards the ideational content, but, as we will show below, the proto-type of affirmation is present in the drive.

On the semantic level, "affirmation" is the antonym of negation. Both the "affirmative" and the "negative" belong in the Aristotelian category of ὀνόματα ἀοριστά, by which term Aristotle designates abstractions. They contrast with the real ονοματα, which he calls φωναὶ σημαντικαὶ, that is, real name words.

On the logical level, negation cannot arise without the previous existence of a content or an assent. It is predicated on the *a priori* existence of affirmation. This definition sum-marizes the views of the great majority of philosophical schools from Aristotle to Sigward. We will disregard for our purposes the special position taken by Heidegger and his followers. The affirmative, by contrast, is not predicated logically on the prior existence of a negative.

In psychoanalytic theory affirmation carries a connotation of its own. Affirmation is the essential attribute of instinct. No conscious counterpart, no ideational content is required to elicit the appetitive properties (Glover, 1943) of the drive which are manifested in its directional quality. We will speak, therefore, of drive manifestations in archaic behavior, like rooting and other discharge phenomena, as being "affirmative."

[104]

This usage of the term is the corollary of Freud's statement that "No" does not exist in the unconscious. We believe that we are justified to infer that, when Freud states that "No" does not exist in the unconscious, he also implies that the quality of the drive is "Yes." But we would qualify our inference from Freud's statement as follows: when unopposed, the quality of the drive is "Yes."

The tacit assumption that the stimulus barrier represents such an opposing force is misleading. I have stated elsewhere that the stimulus barrier is neither an obstacle, nor does it express refusal. It is the manifestation of a maturational state, namely, that at birth the sensorium is not yet cathected. In other terms, the pathways to and from the sensorium are not operative, they do not yet function; accordingly, the drive discharge is undirected and diffuse. The stimulus barrier does not belong in the same conceptual category as negation and affirmation.

The stimulus barrier is a physiological aspect of drive-energy distribution and of the organization of afferent and efferent pathways. Affirmation and negation are the mental epiphenomena of processes of cathectic shifts between the ego and the id. The stimulus barrier functions at the level of the primary process. Affirmation and negation are operations on the level of the secondary process. The stimulus barrier recedes progressively as the pathways mature and the sensory receiving stations become energized. Concomitantly, development can implement the cathexis of the receiving centers in the psychic apparatus.

We will use the term "affirmation" in our further discussion to include: (1) on the archaic level of nondifferentiation the directional quality of drive and discharge, as well as what we like to call "reception" and "taking into"; (2) on the level of object relations, the "striving toward"; (3) on

[105]

the ideational level the meaning of concurring, assenting, accepting and affirming; (4) and finally, on the semantic level, "affirmation" is manifested by the word "Yes" and by the head-nodding gesture. In terms of Freud's discussion of nega- tion, the affirmative judgment asserts that a thing has a par- ticular property or affirms that a particular presentation exists in reality.

With this we have presented our concept of the ideational content of affirmation. It remains to be seen whether our explanation will yield further information on the genetic line which leads to the eventual achievement of the ideational meaning of "Yes."

We will now proceed to examine the motor pattern of the "Yes" gesture. Could the head-nodding "Yes" gesture have developed suddenly at the semantic level in the second year of life, as the obverse of head-shaking, through a transposi- tion of the head-shaking movement from the horizontal into the vertical plane? The two would then come to signify opposites. That would be a very unconvincing explanation; it is true that the two gestures are clearly distinguishable from each other, but so would be a number of other possible movements of the head.

Our genetic bias encourages us to examine the data of direct infant observation in the hope of finding forerunners of the motor pattern of the "Yes" gesture. After all, we have found in the case of the "No" gesture that its motor pattern is preformed already at birth and firmly anchored in phylo- genesis. Our conclusion that the quality of the drive is affirmative makes it even more plausible that the "Yes" ges- ture also should have such remote precursors in onto- and phylogenesis. However, such does not seem to be the case. In the inventory of the newborn's behavior patterns head- nodding movements cannot be found.

What then can be the motor prototype for the head-nodding "Yes" gesture? We find it used by toddlers, probably very soon after the head-shaking "No" has been acquired.

For a long time we were unable to discover anything about the origin of the head-nodding "Yes" gesture. We had to rest satisfied with the obvious, namely that head-nodding could not be as early a pattern as head-shaking because of anatomical considerations. Muscular development and consequently the strength of the newborn's neck muscles are not adequate to support the head in a head-nodding movement. It is only in the third month that the newborn in the supine position becomes capable of lifting his head from the pillow. On the other hand, the neck musculature is adequate from the beginning for rooting movements, if the head is supported. In the experiments performed by Tilney and Casamajor (1924), by Tilney and Kubie (1931), and recently by Prechtl (1952), the newborn kittens were placed on a horizontal surface which supports their heads. In these experiments phylogenetic prototypes for the rooting movement were evident, but none for head-nodding. As we were later to discover, there does exist such a prototype.

We began to achieve an understanding of the head-nodding behavior after we subjected our motion picture material on nursing infants to a searching re-examination. In our study of nursing infants we had consistently made use of an experiment which Margaret Fries (1947) had suggested for the purposes of examining the newborn's activity patterns on one hand, his reaction to frustrations on the other. A similar experiment had been used previously by Rippin and Hetzer (1930) to test the newborn's perceptual development.

The experiment consists in placing the breast-fed baby into the nursing situation. The baby is then offered the nipple and permitted to nurse. After sixty seconds the nipple

[107]

is withdrawn for a period of sixty seconds and subsequently restored to the baby. The baby's behavior in accepting and taking the nipple, his reaction to nipple withdrawal and to the return of the nipple is observed.

We performed this experiment on all infants whose breast feeding we were permitted to investigate, and in each case we filmed the whole sequence. In the re-examination of these motion pictures we noticed an instructive behavior pattern during the nipple withdrawal interval in the case of one of our older infants. The infant in question is Case No. CC 25 (age 0;3 + 17). When after one minute's nursing the nipple was removed, this infant performed repeated approach movements to the breast with her head. These approach movements of the head are phenotypically identical with the semantic nodding gesture of "Yes."

Further investigation showed that this head-nodding approach does not arise suddenly. Two successive stages could be distinguished in its development, the second of which we have just described. The earlier stage, which we will call the precursor phase, is of particular interest, as its metamorphosis into the later phase throws some light on the vicissitudes of behavior patterns which eventually become a vehicle of communication.

We observed the precursor phase in Case No. 17 (age 0;1 + 19). Infants at this age cannot nod their heads unless it is supported. The motion picture shows No. 17 nursing, his head pillowed on the mother's breast. In the process of nursing his head performs forward and backward nodding motions. These follow the rhythm of his sucking movements. Closer scrutiny shows that the head movements are due more or less to mechanical causes. When No. 17 performs a strong sucking movement, his head is pulled forward. When he stops the sucking to swallow, his head falls backward. Anyone familiar with large numbers of breast-fed infants in their first months will recognize this typical picture of vigorous sucking.

It would then appear that an infant six weeks older, like No. 25, who could already support her head with the help of the neck musculature, responds to the withdrawal of the nipple by striving to approach what she had lost. The infant wanted to get the nipple back in the mouth; quite consciously, we can say, as she was already three months old. She performed the approach movements which had served so well while she was sucking. But now the approach did not carry far enough, she was unable to reach the nipple. Her head falls back and she repeats this cycle again and again until the nipple is restored to her. The motor pattern which results from this action is similar to the head-nodding "Yes" in the adult.

The history of the head-nodding movement is somewhat different from that of the head-shaking movement. Head-shaking rooting is an innate biological pattern with a long history reaching into phylogenesis. Head-nodding is not innate. The physical apparatus to perform it is potentially available. But the pattern itself arises in ontogenesis. However, it does not begin for psychological motives, but for mechanical reasons. It is only in the course of the vicissitudes of development after three months that psychological motives will make use of head-nodding for their own purposes.

Our finding that head-nodding, which arises from the very action of sucking, ultimately becomes a vehicle of communication would seem to contradict the assumption I voiced in Chapter VIII (pp. 65-66) . There I suggested that consummatory behavior leads to object relations, while communication originates from approach behavior. There can be no question that the head-nodding of No. 17, (age 0;1 $+$ 19) is part of her consummatory behavior. But that holds true only of the motor pattern during the *precursor* phase of head-nodding. Six weeks later, when musculature has become strong enough to support the head freely, as shown in case No. 25, the same motor pattern is used as an approach behavior. This change of function was effected by the child's striving to re-create the consummation of need gratification. Indeed, as we will discuss below, at this age level head-nodding is the approach behavior par excellence.

It appears then that both head-shaking and head-nodding are primarily approach behaviors. As such they lend themselves in situations of deprivation to the hallucinatory evocation of the action leading to satiation. This is quite similar to the clinical picture of traumatic neuroses. There the situation immediately preceding the trauma is re-created as if in an attempt to undo trauma, loss, deprivation.

On the other hand, head-nodding has been transformed in the fourth month of life from a consummatory into an approach behavior, which means that it has become a detour behavior. That makes it suitable to become ultimately a vehicle of communication, just as we have shown in the case of the detour behavior of rooting.

We mentioned above that head-nodding between the third and the sixth month of life is the approach behavior par excellence. We have a motion picture of a third, somewhat older infant, who was bottle fed. In this infant the approach movements of the head toward the bottle, which had been withdrawn, are combined with reaching out of the hands (Priv. No. 4; age 0;5 + 8). Finally, we could establish that grasping in the prone position begins with what Katherine Wolf has called "mouth-grasping" and in the prone position takes the form of nodding movements of the head toward the desired object.

[110]

These observational documents demonstrate that there does exist a prototype behavior for nodding movements in the nursing situation. Obviously the phenomenon could only be detected in older nurslings who had already achieved mastery of the head-supporting neck muscles. This was the reason why we had not noticed this behavior previously—in our nursing observations, older breast-fed nurslings were in the minority.

At the same time we realized immediately that this nodding behavior of the nursling in front of the breast has a familiar phylogenetic parallel in a precocial, the calf, and probably in many other precocial mammals. The parallel behavior consists in the repetitive head-butting of the nursing calf against the udder, which we have described earlier. This tends in a way to support Portmann's (1951, 1956) proposition that man is a precocial who has deviated into altricial patterns.

This parallel sheds further light on the question why there are no head-nodding movements in the human newborn or in other altricial mammals at birth. In the precocial calf the releaser stimulus for nursing behavior is a visual percept. Altricial mammals, however, at birth are incapable of visual perception, over and beyond the fact that their neck musculature is still inadequate to support their heads for the purposes of a head-nodding movement.

Precocials, on the contrary, have to support their heads freely from the beginning and have the appropriate neck musculature. Furthermore, visual orientation (if not necessarily discrimination) is present in the precocial from birth. Accordingly, beginning with birth, the releaser stimulus for the precocial calf is a visual one, namely any large *moving* object; it walks toward it and hits against it.

By the time the altricial human infant is three months old,

[111]

he also perceives visually, for he responds to the smiling adult's face by smiling himself. At this time, furthermore, his neck musculature has developed to the point where he can lift his head freely. Consequently, in the three-months-old, visual perception combines with mastery of the neck musculature.

We have presented above a series of infant observations of early head-nodding behavior. In all of these, head-nodding approach was only performed when the infant could both see and reach the desired object (rattle, milk bottle, breast). We may state, therefore, that mastery of the neck musculature and of visual perception are the necessary, though not the sufficient, conditions for head-nodding behavior. Hence, the three-months-old, from whose mouth the breast has just been removed but still remains in reach, will perform the head-nodding approach movements in trying to regain the nipple.

The head movements in the three-months-old child have the same function as the butting movements which the precocial calf performs from birth, as soon as it stands on its feet. This function is approach. From the beginning the calf is able to perceive visually and to perform coordinated approach movements. The infant, who is an altricial, reaches the inception of this stage only after the third month.[1]

[1] In the light of the considerations which we have elaborated elsewhere, we may assume that perceptually the infant is probably on a somewhat different level in the third month from that of the precocial calf. This level is partly more, partly less primitive. For the three-months-old baby has already learned to perceive diacritically a few elementary structural details in the nodding human face. The newborn calf's perception, however, is unlearned; I believe that it recognizes only the movement and not the diacritic detail of the large moving object. *Any* large moving object which moves across its visual field will cause the newborn calf to walk toward it. When the calf has reached the large moving object, it performs the further approach actions with the help of tactile orientation.

We assume that the head-nodding approach movements of the three-months-old infant, from whom the mother withdraws the nipple, are only partially governed by the visual perception of either breast or nipple. Our motion pictures show that when the nipple is suddenly withdrawn from the mouth, the infant's eyes shift from the mother's face and, without focusing specifically on the breast, deviate more or less in its general direction. The breast is not fixated by the infant's eye, but its image is probably present in the peripheral parts of the retina, together with the face.

It appears likely that when we performed this experiment, the "cavity perception" of the nipple was interrupted by the loss of the nipple and followed within the same second by the visual presence of the breast adding itself to that of the face. This withdrawal of the nipple does not occur only in the experimental situation, but takes place in a more or less modified form at practically every feeding. I am unwilling to assume that at this age level the infant connects these events. But there is certainly an unbroken transition present from the quasi-coenesthetic cavity perception of the nipple to the peripheral vision of the breast plus face, which may lure the infant to follow it with his head movements.

This is a sequence of discrete events. Perhaps they are experienced as a continuity, or as a single event, a unit by the infant. To us it suggests something more than this. We believe, that this sequence—cavity perception (of the nipple), unpleasure (upon the loss of the nipple), peripheral vision of breast plus face—plays a decisive role in that it expedites the infant's dawning awareness of the separateness of the "I" and the "non-I."

In this primal awareness "I" is what one *feels inside;* "non-I" is what one can *only see* after having lost what one felt inside. It would seem that it is from this loss, and from

[113]

the wishful fantasy attached to what one can only see, that the dream screen described by Lewin is derived.

The function of the dream screen would be analogous to that of the last percept preceding amnesia in traumatic neurosis. Re-experiencing this last percept precipitates the recurrence of the attack; it is as if the traumatic neurotic were attempting to repeat the traumatic experience in an effort to achieve a happier outcome; as if the catastrophe could be wiped out by undoing. It is as if the dreamer would re-establish the dream screen to get the nipple back into the mouth.

The proposition that "I" is what one *feels* inside, while "non-I" is what one *sees* outside, finds some support in direct observation. We have observed at the same age level, in the third and fourth month, the so-called "experimental movements" in the majority of normally developed infants. These are slow, flowing, deliberate movements of hands and fingers which the three-months-old performs, holding his hands at arm's length before his eyes, staring at the movements of his fingers with concentrated attention. One gets the impression that the child is learning to coordinate finger movements by performing them under visual control. This behavior can be observed for several weeks, during which this is one of the favorite occupations of the child. However, these apparent "exercises in directed finger control" do not result in a conspicuous improvement of the child's grasping performance. That will come two or three months later; and fine finger-grasping appears eight months later. Therefore, the function of these "exercises" appears to be a different one.

That is borne out by an experiment which I made on a few such children. When they were in the middle of the finger movements and staring at their moving fingers, I interposed a piece of cardboard, taking care not to let this touch the child, in such a manner that the child could not see his hands. The finger movements continued uninterrupted. We may presume that the child continued to experience proprioceptive messages from the movements of his hands. One may ask oneself whether these movements performed by the child were not in the service of distinguishing the "I" from the "non-I," that is, proprioception from visual distance perception, rather than an attempt to master any kind of muscular coordination.

Distinguishing the "I" from the "non-I" is the *conditio sine qua non* of directed communication. Before there is any reason for directed communication to emerge, awareness of another being, distinct from the subject, must be established. The child acquires this awareness in response to the need-satisfying human face; to that of the mother; but at this period the awareness is not sufficient to enable the child to perceive the need satisfier as a total person. From this rudimentary incomplete awareness of the other person a long line of development leads to the awareness of the self.

In the previous chapters it has become evident that we make a rather rigorous distinction between the "ego," the "I," and the "self." The definition of the ego was given by Freud when he introduced the concept of psychic structure. Among the ego's functions is that of a central steering organization, mediating between the outside and the rest of the psyche. The "I" and the "non-I" are nonanalytic concepts. They were introduced by us to describe phenomena normally occurring and empirically observed in infants. These terms denote the subject's incipient awareness of there being "something separate" from him. At this stage this "something separate" is the surround. This awareness arises through a progressive restriction of the newborn's primary narcissism by the onset of rudimentary ego functions, foremost among which is perception. Kubie (1953), in clinical work with adults, has developed a rather similar concept of "I" and "non-I," with the difference that he considers the "I" as an "apperceptive mass" in the sense of William James. In my concept, based on work with infants, the development of apperception is both later and secondary to the development of rudimentary perception.

It remains to define the "self," to describe how it originates and becomes established. This, to my knowledge, has never been done explicitly in psychoanalytic literature and will be the subject of the next chapter.

12.

The Self and the Ego

For the past ten years psychoanalytic authors have increasingly used the term "the self" in its phenomenological meaning. Freud, when speaking of the self on various occasions, used the term "ego." This was pointed out by Hartmann (1950) who at the same time emphasized that in the paper "On Narcissism" Freud introduced the criteria for a distinction between the self and the object as well as between the self and the ego. References to the self in one form or another become more frequent in Freud's later writings, and in his last paper, the *Outline of Psychoanalysis* (1939), he describes self-preservation as a function of the ego.

In the rest of the psychoanalytic literature the self was rarely distinguished from the ego and hardly ever defined. Until very recently the enormous area opened up, first by Freud's discovery of the unconscious, and later by his massive reformulations of theory in terms of psychic structure and of the dual instinct theory, absorbed the interest of psychoanalysts to the detriment of such apparently secondary questions as those pertaining to the self.

It might be assumed that the increasingly frequent exchanges with investigators in other fields of science have aroused psychoanalytic interest in the concept of the self. However, in my belief it is much more the analytic exploration of the preschool child under the leadership of Anna Freud which gradually compelled analysts to distinguish between self and ego. An equally important influence for the investigation of the self originates in the extensive work on psychosis done in the United States. The contribution of Edith Jacobson (1954) is an outstanding example in this respect.

On the purely theoretical level, Bernfeld (1925) discussed the findings of experimental infant psychologists in terms of psychoanalytic theory. However, the results were meager. For the narrow conceptual framework of experimental psychology in the 1920's precluded findings which might have been relevant for psychoanalytic insight. This was the consideration which induced me to undertake direct infant observation oriented by psychoanalytic principles, beginning in 1935. The subject under investigation in direct infant observation is preverbal behavior, in contrast to psychoanalytic therapy, which operates largely with verbal behavior. Nonverbal behavior, primarily motor behavior, is instrumental in distinguishing the self from the environment (Hartmann, Kris, Loewenstein, 1946). Therefore, the observation of the infant's preverbal behavior alerted the investigator to the differences between the ego and the self. A progressively clear definition of the conceptual differences between ego and self emerged from the thorough study of the role of the ego in adaptation, of its apparatuses and functions (Hartmann, 1939), from the findings on intrasystemic processes and conflicts (Hartmann, 1950), from the distinction between the synthetic (Nunberg, 1931), the organizing (Hartmann, 1939), and the integrative function (Kris, 1956) of the ego. In this context we have already mentioned the work of Jacobson (1954), in connection with her findings in the analyses of adult psychotics. Equally extensive are the contributions of

Margaret Mahler in connection with her work on psychotic children (1952, 1955). Recently Hartmann (1955) and Kris (1955) have taken up the problems of the self in terms of the distribution and shifts of cathexis.

In my own studies of infants, I have until very recently refrained from discussing the self. In the first place, in my opinion, and as I will show later in this chapter, the self has its inception around the fifteenth month of life. In this I disagree with Jacobson (1954) who assumes that the self cannot be clinically discerned in the first two years. Furthermore, my attention was absorbed by the ontogenesis of the ego and the unfolding of object relations. I feel now that my observations have progressed to the point in the development of the child where self-awareness becomes discernible and an integrated view of the genesis of the self becomes available.

As I see it, the self is the product of awareness. It is the subject's awareness that he is a sentient and acting entity, separate and distinct from objects and environment. But awareness, an ego function, goes through a number of developmental stages, of which in the present study we have only reached the one in which self-awareness can be demonstrated.

The system ego has its inception as a body ego in the third month of life. It is at that stage a steering and control organization, which performs its functions with the help of beginning awareness and beginning neuromuscular coordination.

It can be proved experimentally that at this stage the subject is aware of percepts outside of him, but not that the ego is aware of the subject as acting sentient entity. If awareness of the own body could be demonstrated already, this would be the body self (Anna Freud, 1953; Glover, 1924). But even then I would be somewhat reluctant to speak of the self at this stage. I conceive of the self as an ideational elaboration of emotional and somatic experience, predicated on the realization of separateness, of being an individual. At the three-months stage primary narcissism is dominant, the sense of separateness and the capacity for ideation are nonexistent. I have therefore avoided the term self in discussing this stage and have spoken of the awareness of a "non-I" without asuming any awareness of the "I."

I believe that the conclusions now reached in our exploration of the ontogenesis of semantic communication also permit us to present a coherent report on the genesis of selfawareness. In what follows, we will attempt to explore this process and the differentiation of the self from the objects in the context of the development of semantic communication in the child. As a preliminary, let us outline briefly *the relations between the "I," the "ego" and the "self."*

We consider the "I," like later on the self, to be a product of the awareness of the ego. We have described above what we believe to be the precursor of the "I," namely the infant's awareness of a "non-I." This emerges at the three-months level. The infant works out in the subsequent three to six months an awareness of the "I" in virtue of actions performed in his relations with the "non-I."

The "I," therefore, is to be conceived as a cognitive precipitate of experience. In contrast to this, the ego as a system is a construct of psychoanalytic theory.

The Self and Its Origins

The self is also a cognitive precipitate of experience, on a higher level of integration than the "I." Chronologically, the awareness of the self begins around fifteen months of life, about one year after the inception of the awareness of a "non-I." Genetically, the self can be traced to the "I," while the "I" originates from the infant's emotionally cathected physical relations with the "non-I."

The self, which is a continuation of the "I" on a higher level, is the product of intrapsychic processes which take place as a result of the vicissitudes of object relations. In the precursor stage of object relations, the object was a constituent part of the "non-I," out of which it is segregated step by step, beginning as part object. It achieves the dignity of love object as a result of emotional interchanges which develop progressively into true object relations.

These relations are mediated through the functioning of the ego; in their turn, in a circular process, they call forth in the ego a structuration of ever-increasing complexity, which achieves effectiveness through its progressive integration. The ego implements these relations through the instrumentality of the "I." In the course of this process the "I" accumulates cathectic charges. The ever-increasing cathectic investment finally compels the ego to become aware of the "I's" function in the unfolding object relations. *Through this awareness of the ego the "I" now achieves identity as the self.*

The self, even in the adult, always shows traces of its origin. For its origin is on the one hand closely connected to the body and to its functions (Schilder, 1935), on the other to the exchanges in the course of object relations. This double origin, the narcissistic and the social one, can be traced in all our references to the self, e.g., self-regard, self-sufficiency, self-importance, etc. All self-awareness combines the ego's awareness of one's own person, tinged with the consciousness of the "other's" reaction to it. This is already adumbrated by Freud (1914) in his observation that "part of the self-regard is primary—the residue of childish narcissism; another part arises out of such omnipotence as experience corroborates (the fulfillment of the ego ideal), whilst a

[121]

third part proceeds from the gratification of object libido."[1]

The steps which lead to the emergence of the self consist in successive phases of increasing differentiation within the psyche and of the subject's increasing awareness of his separateness from the surround. No such awareness exists in the first of these phases at the three-months level, at which the world of the child is divided into "I" and "non-I." As we have shown by experiments, no distinction is made between animate and inanimate surround as long as both possess certain primitive Gestalt attributes.

The next step occurs when a difference is made between the living surround and the inanimate world. This discrimination begins in the course of the second half of the first year, around the eighth month of life, when the child becomes able to distinguish the libidinal object from strangers. The eight-months anxiety marks the beginning of object relations proper and sets the stage for the incipient awareness of the self. The differentiation of the "I" from the "non-I" establishes the separateness of the subject from the surround. The beginning of object relations proper establishes the mother as love object and therefore as separate from the subject. Paradoxically, these relations could be called a defense against a growing awareness of separateness. When the child is gradually and progressively deprived of bodily closeness and skin contact, he replaces them by forming emotional ties.

On the other hand, the child's growing autonomy and wish for independence make him ever more sharply aware of his separateness in the following six months. This culminates in the child's turning the device achieved through "identification with the aggressor" against the libidinal ob-

[1] See also Hartmann (1950): "We define narcissism as the libidinal cathexis, not of the ego, but of the self"; as well as Kris (1956, pp. 449-452).

ject around the fifteenth month of life. The manifest indicator of this event is the child's use of "No" (in gesture and word), which he has appropriated from the adult. It becomes instrumental not only in elaborating further the separateness between child and adult, but also in objectivating the child's own self.

Centrifugal and Centripetal Tendencies

This tendency to separateness counteracts from the beginning the child's more obvious tendency of clinging to the mother. The simultaneous presence of diametrically opposed tendencies in the child, beginning with birth, cannot be sufficiently emphasized. They have their exact counterpart in the existence of similar tendencies in the mother. With the cutting of the umbilical cord, a cleavage takes place between mother and child. They become discrete physical entities. At the same time, as if driven by a desperate urge to re-establish the previous state, both mother and child strive for as close a contact as possible with each other, culminating in the nursing act. But at the end of nursing they are driven apart again, a cycle which is recaptured with each nursing act. In *Weaning* (1947), a motion picture, I have shown how at the end of the nursing act the mother of a five-months-old, when the child has abandoned the nipple and fallen asleep, clutches him again and again to her breast, unable to endure the parting.

The repetitive frustrations, imposed by the delays between need and consummation of the child's wish to nurse, enforce the differentiation of the "non-I" from the "I." This establishes the infant as a discrete *psychological* entity, about three months after the severance of the umbilical cord had established him as a discrete *physical* entity.

In opposition to this centrifugal current, which increases

the chasm between mother and child, is the child's vital need and wish for the mother. Freud (1914) described the dynamics of this antithetical process in the following words: "The development of the ego consists in a departure from the primary narcissism and results in a vigorous attempt to recover it."

From the viewpoint of earliest object relations we must never lose sight of this circular process in which the diametrically opposite tendencies of the child, to cling and to cleave, are mirrored by the equally conflicting strivings of the mother, to embrace and to remove. Under normal circumstances, in the first few months, the mother's antithetic tendencies are in harmonious interaction with the antithetic tendencies in the child. With the increase in the child's autonomy the synchronicity of child and mother is subjected to ever more frequent disturbances. Such asynchronous incidents, as well as the attempts from both sides to re-establish synchronicity, contribute greatly to the richness of the developing object relations.

In the beginning the correspondence between the mother's and the child's urges finds its expression in the greater or lesser closeness of bodily contact. As mentioned elsewhere, in some preliterate societies this closeness of immediate skin contact is an extraordinarily important factor in insuring the secure unfolding of the infant's development. Anna Freud has pointed out what an important role the lack of skin contact plays in the etiology of later disturbances. Ashley Montagu (1950, 1953) presented evidence of the importance of the earliest skin contact for survival in mammals. I have repeatedly expressed the opinion that throughout the Western world skin contact betwen mother and child has been progressively and artificially reduced in an attempted denial of the importance of mother-child relations, probably with damaging results for future generations.

But be the relation and the contact ever so close, the centrifugal tendencies inherent in the baby's maturation and in the mother's feelings—not to speak of the eventual cessation of lactation—inevitably enforce weaning and physical separateness. It cannot be accidental that this coincides chronologically so frequently with the stage at which the baby becomes able to distinguish the mother from the stranger, that is, to conceive of her as a person whom he recognizes among all others.[2]

Object Relations Proper

This is the point at which I situate the beginning of true object relations, of object relations proper. This is a proposition which stands and falls, of course, with the way in which we wish to define the term "object relations." For my purpose I have always maintained that the minimal prerequisite for true object relations is the existence of a reasonably integrated and organized ego, concomitantly with the capacity to distinguish the libidinal object from all other persons in the world.

The relations which precede the establishment of true object relations are much more in the nature of crude need gratification. That does not preclude such relations from being of a very intricate nature. Their requirements are

2 I do not wish to imply that weaning at six months of age is in any way a universal phenomenon. But weaning in the second half of the first year is a frequent one, not only in our culture. Even if weaning is not complete, an increasing measure of sucking frustration is imposed (statistically speaking) on infants in all cultures at this period through external necessity, be that the need for the mother to work in the field, the mother's next pregnancy, or similar reasons. And we would suspect that, when weaning is postponed, a certain (though not unlimited) delay will occur in the infant's psychic development.

[125]

frequently not easily satisfied, and replacing them can present major problems. But this is equally true in the case of well-established conditioned reflexes. Yet these difficulties are as nothing compared to those which will arise when true object relations have been established, and we may ask ourselves wherein the difference lies.

In my opinion, the crude need gratification of the period of preobjectal relations (ranging from nursing to body and skin contact) involves rather simple elements relatively easy to produce and reproduce. But object relations proper fuse immediate need gratification with emotional and psychological interchange; these form the weft and the woof of highly individual emotional ties. These cannot be replaced when broken. New ones have to be formed—an extremely difficult task. It requires the compliance of both mother substitute and child. The two have to go through the inchoate and inarticulate preliminaries which lead in the normal infant to the development of preobjectal relations and from there to the formation of true object relations. This process requires unlimited patience and unfailing empathy on the part of the mother substitute. In the recent experiments with the so-called "anaclitic therapy" (Margolin, 1954), a first attempt has been made to implement the insights gained from child observation in the therapy of adults. Therapeutically interested analysts undoubtedly will realize the implications of our propositions on the origins of communication for therapy.

We have proceeded in our argument from the point where mother and child became discrete *physical* entities after the delivery, to their becoming discrete *psychological* entities after the division of the "I" from the "non-I"; the next step occurs in the third quarter of the first year, when body and skin contacts grow rarer and are replaced by emotional ties.

The progressive development of these emotional ties over the following six months, their dynamic processing with the help of the identification with the aggressor, leads to the establishment of the self. The infant, who, from a discrete physical entity, has become a discrete psychological entity, is finally established as a *discrete social unit,* as a person, through the confrontation of the self and the non-self, namely, "the other."

There are a number of striking parallels between the ontogenesis of the self and that of the differentiation between the "I" and the "non-I." In both cases frustration plays a major role. The child is forced to distinguish the "I" from the "non-I" on the three-months level because of the frustration of his oral needs when he desires the breast. Similarly, the fifteen-months-old is forced to become aware of the difference between the self and "other" because of the frustration imposed on his volition[3] by the libidinal object's "No."

Another parallel in the development of the two is evident when we view it from the perspective of objectivation. When the "I" is differentiated from the "non-I," there is an awareness of the "non-I," but no awareness of the "I." Similarly, when the libidinal object is constituted at the eight-months level, there is a manifest and demonstrable awareness of the object, but no demonstrable awareness of the self. This is achieved only in the course of the following six months, as a result of affective exchanges within the framework of object relations.

In terms of development both events are progressive in that each on its own level imposes an increased compliance with the reality principle. The inception of the functioning

3 Volition: The act of deciding on a course of action and initiating it (Warren, 1935). See also Hartmann (1939).

of the reality principle is evident at the three-months level, when the hungry infant becomes able to suspend the urge for the immediate gratification of his oral need. He does so for the time necessary to perceive the mother's face and to react to it. This is the developmental step in which the "I" is differentiated from the "non-I"; in which the infant becomes aware of the "otherness" of the surround. The delay in gratification is made possible by the functioning of the reality principle, which in this phase is acquired through maturation, combined with the unfolding and organizing of conscious perception and of memory traces laid down in the wake of affective relations with the need-gratifying object.

In the course of the following twelve months an ever-increasing number of ego systems and ego functions come under the sway of the reality principle. When at fifteen months the child differentiates the self from the "other," he must in addition take over some of the functions of the love object. These are the functions which the libidinal object performed in its capacity of the child's external ego, e.g., that of being the child's executive in the field of locomotion, of entertaining the child, etc. Less evident, though more important is the libidinal object's role in performing reality testing for the child. This means that the child now comes into collision, literally, with more and more of the hard facts of reality. Previously mother carried him from one room into the other, unscathed, at a reasonable speed. Now he runs too fast, loses his balance and hits his head painfully against the door-jamb. Such experiences force him to begin to "evaluate" (Jacobson, 1954) his capacities of locomotion, of balance, of depth perception—in one word, the limitations of his physical self. He is forced to relate one part of his person after the other to the surround, thus expanding the scope of his

[128]

thought processes and concomitantly of his psychic functions. Collisions of a different nature confront him in the field of emotions. The results are similar, except that the re-evaluation has to take place by relating himself to the "other."

Thus the objectivation of the self goes hand in hand with the objectivation of the "other." With this a new era of reality testing begins. The new autonomy, based on the self-reliance imparted to the child by his use of the "No" against the adult, also makes mandatory the use of judgment and decision for his every action. Judgment is a function which can only be applied with the help of constantly re-iterated reality testing. This leads to an extensive development, enrichment and reinforcement of ego systems, ego functions and ego apparatuses. We will therefore formulate the following propositions:

The acquisition of the "No" is the indicator of a new level of autonomy, of the awareness of the "other" and of the awareness of the self; it is the beginning of a restructuration of mentation on a higher level of complexity; it initiates an extensive ego development, in the framework of which the dominance of the reality principle over the pleasure principle becomes increasingly established.

The direction taken by this ego development becomes further evident in the role-playing games which begin characteristically in the course of the first half of the second year, somewhere around fifteen months of age. In these the child diapers his doll, feeds her from a bottle, puts her to bed and uses the "No" gesture to the doll.[4] A measure of self-awareness is evident in these performances. It is even more obvious when, as we mentioned on page 48, the child uses the "No"

4 Anna Freud (1952) describes this identification with the mother at a later age: deprived of a mother's care, the sick child "plays mother and child" with his own body.

to himself while he is playing a make-believe game of doing something forbidden.

In these games a cleavage between ego and self is evident. The restructured ego has objectivated the self by taking it as an object.[5] The ego applies here the same device to the self which it had learned to apply against the mother, namely the "No." It had learned to use this device with the help of identification with the aggressor; this led to an increasing objectivation of the mother. Now using the "No" in his games will lead to an increasing objectivation of the self.

We spoke of the shift of cathexis which takes place in the course of identifying with the aggressor. In this mechanism, passive submission to unpleasure is replaced by active aggression. This restructuration has an ideational counterpart, namely the first emergence of the capacity of abstraction. It is probable that shifts of aggressive cathexis are responsible for a number of mental operations, among them that of abstraction.

The beginning awareness of the self is predicated on the awareness of the "other." An unmistakable testimony of this self-awareness is provided around eighteen months, when the child begins to speak of himself in the third person.

Recapitulation

To facilitate the reader's task in following the intricate interplay between psychic energies and the actual experiences leading to the acquisition of the "No," we will recapitulate the givens: (1) the child's congenital equipment, which includes the capacity to form object relations; (2) the maturational process; (3) the developmental process. This last one involves two distinct aspects: (a) object relations, (b) the endopsychic processes of the child. The child's con-

---

[5] See Hartmann (1939) on objectivation as a function of the ego.

genital equipment is the focus of a field of forces created by shifting object relations. These object relations produce reverberations in the child's endopsychic processes leading to shifts of cathexis, to the formation of psychic structures, which in their turn interact in a circular process with the force field of ever-changing object relations. In short, the achievement of negation is the result of an interaction between the child's object relations and his endopsychic processes. The child's use of "No" in gesture or word indicates that this has been accomplished.

We will now discuss the nature of the extensive changes which occur concomitantly in object relations as well as in the child's endopsychic structure and dynamics.

A Grade in Object Relations

When the child uses mentation to express aggression against the libidinal object, he acquires at the same time a new vehicle for his object relations. This vehicle is semantic communication.

Semantic communication opens the door from the private sphere of archaic object relations to the wider sphere of social relations. The result is an extraordinary enrichment through the introduction of a new dimension into the mother-child relations. Libidinal and aggressive drives had hitherto been discharged in the framework of object relations through direct volitional muscular action. Now ideational processes are interposed, judgment comes into play, a choice between "No" and "Yes" is made. In the place of direct muscular action a new function becomes available: the use of "No" *against* the libidinal object. *This momentous step introduces the alternative of discussion in place of attack, an achievement only to be found in humans. Thus, social intercourse in humans can begin.*

[131]

The capacity to use mental operations and to communicate them through verbal symbols instead of having to act, instead of having recourse to fight or flight, confers a new measure of autonomy on the child. This measure of autonomy is either concomitant with, or results in, the incipient awareness of the self. The child as an independent person, with a will of his own, confronts the "other," who is equally independent, also a discrete person with a will of his own. Prior to the achievement of this autonomy the resources available to the child permitted only straightforward drive discharge according to the pleasure principle by means of muscular action. Now he has an alternative, namely, communication through verbal (or gesture) symbols. This raises object relations from the level of the instinctual drive to the level of social relations.

When it becomes possible to use verbal refusal or assent instead of hate or love, resistance or submission, fight or flight—then the beginning of negotiation and discussion has been made. Action has been displaced by communication on the social level (Nunberg, 1952).

From the vantage point of endopsychic structure and dynamics, we have already discussed the role played by the mechanism of identification with the aggressor. The identification in this case involves much more than only turning aggression outward by taking over the "No" in order to *frustrate the frustrator.*

The libidinal object's role certainly is not limited only to immediately frustrating or hostile intervention; besides all the other aspects of object relations, the libidinal object also functions as the *watcher* or *observer* of the child and as the *executor* of his wishes.

The *watcher* is a new and most important role which the mother has to assume as soon as the baby becomes capable of

[132]

independent locomotion. She has to keep the child under constant observation, so that she can forestall any undesirable activities. We are all aware of the toddler's persistent, and frequently successful, efforts to escape mother's eye. Every mother can be heard to complain loudly about the eternal vigilance which she has to exercise. When the mechanism of "identification with the aggressor" is put into operation, the child will also modify his ego to conform with the mother's function as observer. This is one of the structural and dynamic changes, of which we have spoken above.

The ego in the role of observer[6] will now function in two directions. One is the active, aggressive direction, manifested in the familiar curiosity of the child about the libidinal object, with all its scoptophilic implications and consequences. This process is not at all different from the retaliatory use to which the "No," taken over from the adult, was put; it is simply "tit for tat."

The other direction is centripetal. In identifying with the aggressor, the ego turns the observation against the child himself. In this role the ego takes the self as an object of observation. This self-observation contributes to the progressive ideational objectivation of the self. Our finding on the earliest origins of self-observation is in good agreement with Anna Freud's statement that identification with the aggressor is a preliminary step in the formation of the superego. As we know, one of the superego's most important functions is that of self-observation and evaluation of the self.[7] These two functions of observation are examples of the changes in the child's endopsychic structure, of which we have spoken above.

[6] We are aware that we are using a term introduced by Anna Freud (1936). However, we are using it here in a somewhat different sense from that which she had in mind.
[7] See, however, Hartmann (1953).

On the other hand, the child's becoming the *executor* of his own wishes is a much simpler procedure. Using the current vernacular, one might say that the child adopts the "Do-it-yourself" method. Speaking in psychoanalytic terms, it is the inevitable consequence of the child's turning from passivity to activity which began already around the third month of life. As we have described, the child now is forced to relate himself to his surround through more or less painful collisions with things and persons. In regard to things we may add that maturation has a greater part in this adaptation than dynamic processes. The opposite is the case when the child relates himself to the persons in his surround; object relations have the lion's share in this adaptation.

When the child becomes the executor of his own wishes he also has to become the self-observer which his mother had been. He is now obliged to combine the function of the executor with the function of the watcher. To these functions he must apply a third function, that of judgment. The combination of these three functions will permit him to learn from experience.

In the development of children we take this complicated process for granted; it involves cathectic shifts and mental operations on a relatively low level. Indeed, we can find analogous processes also in the development of the young of the higher mammals, although in these the dynamics are of a different nature.

The existence and the functioning of object relations is the indispensable premise in the building up, in the organization, and in the interaction of these three functions. That in its turn—namely, the interaction of execution, of watching and of judging—is the premise for the laying down of the memory traces required for learning through experience. Donald Hebb (1955), in his experiments on dogs, has impressively shown the indispensableness of object relations in this integration. He raised puppies in solitary confinement, without an opportunity to form object relations, and with a minimum of sensory stimulation. When they grew up, these dogs were, in Hebb's words, ". . . not like ordinary dogs. They are both stupid and peculiar." When grown up, these dogs could not learn from experience. For instance, through five testing periods the dog repeatedly thrust his nose into a lighted match. Hebb demonstrated this incapacity to learn in a film. An "electric hedgehog," which administered electric shocks when touched, was slowly moved close to the dog. Dogs raised in the ordinary way learned after one or two trials to avoid the device with ease. The affect- and stimulation-deprived dogs could not learn this; they became disoriented, went into panic, twirling rapidly around themselves in a narrow circle, like a dog chasing its own tail. The reaction was completely inappropriate and unorganized, in the nature of what Goldstein has called "catastrophic reaction."

Such experiments obviously are out of question with the human. But one is reminded of the results of these experiments when one sees the extraordinary difficulty in learning found in affect-deprived infants. One of their characteristics —and incidentally that of so-called psychopathic or schizophrenic children also—is that they are unable to learn from painful experiences. They can only learn through *gratifying* experiences. It would seem that gratifying experiences open a path for them, however tenuous, to those object relations of which they had been deprived.

To discuss the further changes in the child's personality which result from his relations with love object and social surround would take us beyond the age limits set in the present study. It would involve us in a discussion of the further steps in the formation of language and thought.

Though much work has been done in this area, the processes are not yet sufficiently understood. We will therefore return to the examination of the forces which operate in bringing about the awareness of the self. In particular we will consider what happens at the successive levels of the child's development.

Birth, by separating the child's body from the mother, establishes the child as a discrete *physical* entity. At three months, the child's awareness of the "non-I" is the indicator that he has become a discrete *psychological* entity. Finally the awareness of the self in the second year of life is the indicator that the child has begun to function as a discrete *social* entity. Each of these steps is enforced through frustration. Physical frustration forces the child to become a discrete physical entity. Physical frustrations also transform the child into a psychological entity. By contrast, the child becomes a social entity through psychological frustration.

Each of the three sets of frustrations imposes a progressively increasing compliance with the reality principle. At birth the process of delivery forces the fetus from a vegetative existence to the adaptation of autonomous breathing, of oral food intake, and finally of metabolism.

On the three-months level of the differentiation of the "I" from the "non-I," the delay in the need gratification accelerates the development of perception and of coordinated directed muscular action. With this begins the period in which the infant becomes able to strive volitionally to achieve whatever he wishes.

The Limitation of Volition

Volition and will are terms which appear rarely in psychoanalytic literature.[8] Indeed, it is difficult to find a place for

8 However, see Hartmann (1939, p. 112).

[136]

these terms in the framework of psychoanalytic concepts. When we speak of the drives, we are referring to the unconscious sources of will. On the other hand, its conscious aspect is manifested in the conscious wish. One might find a place for the concept of volition in the antithesis between activity and passivity. It is perhaps due to our disregard of the category of volition in considering this antithesis that repeated unsuccessful attempts have been made to connect activity with masculinity and passivity with femininity.

When the infant develops into a toddler, there is a transitional stage during which manifestations of the child's passing from passivity to activity are conspicuous in every sector of his personality. We believe that in studying this transition the volitional frame of reference is useful. When the child starts on the road to activity, volition inevitably moves into the foreground. We shall examine how, at the turn of the first year, the manifestations of the child's will affect his surround and vice versa.

When toward the end of the first year the child becomes capable of locomotion, the things he can reach, the actions he can perform, are multiplied. Needless to say that all too many of the things he desires are either harmful to him or undesirable for his surround. In this situation the mother has to act as the "frustrating" protector (Anna Freud, 1952). This is a frustration of a different order from those which the child experienced before he had achieved locomotion. At that time, the carrying out of his intentions was primarily frustrated by physical conditions, that is, by the infant's own physical limitations. After he has achieved locomotion, limitations are imposed on the carrying out of his intentions by the persons in his environment. They frustrate his volition and confront him with the limits of his will.

This frustration is infinitely more significant for two reasons: on the one hand the persons who put obstacles in the way of the child's will had been the executors of his wishes before he became capable of locomotion; on the other, these persons who are now frustrating him have become the child's love objects in the course of the development of object relations.

When the mother's role as executor of the child's wishes changes to that of protector against external danger and educator in the ways of life, she is bound to frustrate the child. She inevitably sets up conflicts of will between the child and herself as well as intrapsychic conflicts in the child. The child has achieved erect locomotion and experiences a triumphant feeling of freedom, of independence, of pride of achievement hitherto unknown. That can be shown impressively in motion pictures, e.g., our film record (Priv. No. 2, age 1;0+10). But this triumph is limited; on numberless occasions the child's will conflicts with that of the love object, and more often than not, the child's will is defeated.

Reality Testing and the Formation of the Self

Before he becomes capable of coordinating muscular activity volitionally, the child lives in the realm of infantile omnipotence. His desires (needs) were fulfilled by the environment. When there was a delay in the fulfillment, hallucinatory need gratification stepped in. This was possible because reality testing during the first six months of life is practically nonexistent. Reality testing is predicated on the availability of perception and motility, both of which are either lacking or inadequately developed during that period.

But when directed intentional muscular coordination and after that, around the beginning of the second year, locomotion is achieved, experience imposes on the child a rapid development of reality testing and reality adaptation. During

[138]

the transitional period, the mother acts as the protector of the child and teaches him, step by step, to become his own protector and observer. The clash between the child's will and that of the mother leads the child to recognize the limits of his will, his wishes, his fantasies about himself, and thus the boundaries of the self are narrowed and set up. One may say without exaggeration that the self is fashioned from the atrophied remains of magic omnipotence.

This origin of the self, its linkage with magic omnipotence, will never be completely eradicated and can be traced even in the adult. Reality testing blocks the road of return to the omnipotent origin of the self.

In the normal adult, sleep makes reality testing impossible by eliminating perception. It also makes reality testing unnecessary by arresting motility. The suspension of reality testing unblocks the road of return to the origins of the self; this makes hallucinated need gratification through dreaming possible. A return to the archaic psychic organization which precedes the integration of the self occurs also in psychosis, when the ego function of reality testing is impaired and regression to magic omnipotence becomes evident.

Restriction of Volition and the Anal Phase

We have hardly spoken of another aspect of the development initiated by the achievement of the "No" and will only mention it briefly here. The beginning awareness of the self, the inception of verbal communication, of growing autonomy, of social consciousness, coincides with the onset of the anal phase. At this time begins also the period of stubbornness, in which the refusing "No" plays such a spectacular role.

We can consider this conspicuous role of the refusing "No" as the consequence of the inevitable frustrations imposed on the child's will. These frustrations enforce a perception of the self as a discrete volitional entity through the progressive restriction of the scope of the child's actions. The three-months-old disposes of magic omnipotence; but the jurisdiction of the fifteen-months-old eventually is limited practically to his own body. In the physical sense, the self at this age is identified more or less with this body and when restrictions of the child's will are applied to the body functions, he will wage a last-ditch battle.[9]

For the child, the feces form a part of his own person. Toilet training is resented as an attempt to deprive him of the liberty of using his self, his body, the sphincters. He will defend these liberties stubbornly. This explanation does not exhaust the various aspects of the anal phase. It purports only to show the role of growing self-awareness in the manifestations of stubbornness during the anal phase.

One of these manifestations is the child's repetitive use of the "No" against the adult, even when it does not seem to make sense. We have mentioned the child who says "No" while doing what the adult wishes him to do. It seems to us that this "No" is a manifesto of independence. It is the statement: "I have a will of my own and even when it is the same as yours, it is different because it is my own! I am doing this because *I* want it and I am not doing what *you* want!"

In this example the autistic (dereistic) thinking of the child is very much in evidence. It clearly shows the inappropriate affect, the cleavage[10] between the affect and that which

9 See Anna Freud (1952).

10 The child who communicates his refusal to do something by saying "No" while simultaneously doing it is an early and elementary example of those problems which Hartmann (1951) suggests to study with the help of a "constant scrutiny of intrasystemic synergistic and antagonistic relations." As mentioned, in the second year of life the phenomenon is a normal one. Its pattern is similar to the splitting of the ego during transference (Sterba, 1934) which can also be considered to be within the limits of normality. On the other hand, a path leads from these normal phenomena to the abnormal ones

occasions it. In consequence of this cleavage, the message conveyed by the child contradicts the action he performs. This example shows a behavior which is completely normal for the child in his second year. However, this normal action of the child also throws light on the processes of dereistic thinking and inappropriate affect in schizophrenia.

Organizers of Psychic Development

We have attempted to sketch the extraordinarily wide spectrum of the newly acquired territory which follows the acquisition of the "No." The momentousness of achieving the concept of "No" in the child's development (and in mankind's!) is so great that I feel compelled to revise a statement I have made elsewhere (1954, 1957). I postulated the existence of what I have called "organizers" of the psyche, which mark certain critical stages in the child's psychological and affective development.

This is a proposition which I formulated some twenty-five years ago. At that time I called the developmental levels which separate such critical stages from each other "crucial points" (Spitz, 1934). In the intervening years I have reformulated the concept several times in the light of my observations on large series of infants (1954). Independently of my own work, Bowlby (1953) has come to similar conclusions in regard to factors underlying the development of psychopathic personality. The concept of critical stages of development has also been postulated in animal psychology

---

of the splitting of the ego in the defensive process (Freud, 1938) and to the splitting of the ego along the contours of early introjects in psychosis (Bychowski, 1956). A discussion of the relations and of the differences between these phenomena would require the application of Glover's (1943) careful and constructive distinction between splitting and dissociation. Such an exploration would go beyond the scope of our present study.

by Scott and Marston (1950) and is derived from embryology.[11]

Organizers of the psyche mark certain major levels of personality integration. At such points maturational and developmental processes combine with each other after the manner of an alloy. After such an integration has been achieved, the psychic apparatus functions according to a new and different mode. We have called the product of this integration an "organizer."

The establishment of an organizer of the psyche is revealed by the appearance of specific new behavioral phenomena—symptoms, as it were, of the integration that has taken place. We have, therefore, called these specific behavioral patterns "indicators."

The indicator of the first organizer of the psyche is the appearance of the smiling response. But it should be remembered that this directed intentional smiling of the child is in itself only the visible symptom of the convergence and integration of a number of maturational and psychological trends and events. The emergence of the smiling response, accordingly, is the indicator of the establishment and synthesis of a psychic organization on a higher level of complexity than that which prevailed until then.

The indicator of the second organizer is the phenomenon of the eight-months anxiety. Again, this is only the visible symptom of the underlying major integration and its product. Obviously, the integration of a variety of maturational and developmental processes is predicated on their being in

---

11 Quoting Bowlby (1953): "In embryology it has long been known that the growth of cells is influenced by the particular environment in which they are placed at a particular phase of development. If transplanted before their critical phase, they will grow in a way appropriate to their new environment; but if transplanted after this phase, they will continue to grow in a way appropriate to their original environment. The organization covering their whole future growth is thus determined by their environment in this critical phase."

existence and available to the child at a given period in the individual chronology of the child's life. There is a certain latitude, a number of weeks and perhaps months, within which the integration can take place. Nevertheless, the confluence and integration of the variety of trends is a complicated and, therefore, vulnerable process. In particular, the developmental progress which is dependent on the unfolding of object relations can be delayed. Maturational processes, however, go on regardless of this delay, for they are laid down in the biological Anlage and therefore less subject to environmental influences than development. It is not necessary to discuss here the opposite possibility, that of development which runs ahead of maturation. Glover (1943) dealt with this disturbance which can have similarly undesirable consequences.

Accordingly, if the integration (which produces the organizer) fails to take place, an imbalance of the total personality structure is created. This imbalance results in developmental disturbances and deviations from normality. Once the critical period is passed and a new level reached, the stresses which are set up through asynchronous unfolding of *maturation* and *development* are very difficult to remove. It should not be overlooked either that developmental asynchronicity can also take place in various sectors of the personality itself. The specific clinical pictures resulting from imbalance between maturation and development have hardly been investigated. The same applies to the clinical pictures resulting from imbalance between the different sectors of the psychological personality. We believe that a closer study of the phenomena of developmental and maturational as well as purely developmental imbalance will shed more light on the problem of fixation.

I also suggested that a third organizer is probably indi-

[143]

cated through the establishment of language (in the sense of grown-up speech) around eighteen months of life.

I now wish to qualify this last proposition. I believe that the acquisition of the semantic "No" gesture, which signifies that the child has acquired the faculty of judgment and is becoming aware of the self, is a more specific and more precise indication that the child has reached the stage of the third organizer. I believe that further investigation will show that the achievement of the faculty of judgment on the level of the capacity to signify "No" either by gesture or word will be found to correspond to the achievement of reversibility in terms of Piaget's theory (1936). My revised proposition, therefore, is that the achievement of the head-shaking "No" is the indicator of the establishment of the third organizer.

Communication as an Organizer

The psychic development of the child proceeds as it were through the addition of concentric rings to a rather small initial core. The initial core at birth is the congenital equipment. The first addition consists in the maturation of the perceptive system on one hand, in the development of its cathexis on the other. This enables the child to achieve perception, to initiate relations with the surround, and to differentiate the "I" from the "non-I." The second layer is the differentiation of the animate from the inanimate, concomitantly with the cathexis of the libidinal object, and indicated by the appearance of the eight-months anxiety. Both first and second indicators (smile and eight-months anxiety) operate in terms of action, of turning toward or turning away physically. The third layer consists in the establishment of relations with a surround of non-self nature (in terms of George H. Mead, the "other" and the "generalized other"). The relations with the "generalized other," with the social world, are patterned on the relations with the libidinal object, although the libidinal object remains unique and distinct from the "generalized other." The formation of the third layer is indicated by the acquisition of the semantic "No" and marks the inception of the awareness of the self.

Restated in terms of the organizer concept, the first two organizers belong to the sphere of drive discharge through action; the third organizer initiates *the supremacy of communication which displaces action in an increasing measure.*

From the viewpoint of the individual's energy household it is significant that this advance also results in a saving in energy, while being incomparably more efficient in achieving the individual's aims. Communication is a detour function and, like all detour functions, it operates according to the mode of the reality principle, namely, through the postponement of drive gratification for the purpose of achieving this gratification in a more efficient manner.

I like to think that the new dimension added to object relations by the acquisition of negation was the turning point in man's prehistory. It established man as a species different for all others in regard to the level of his social relations. Animal societies, of course, have their social relations also, some based on action, some on reflex behavior, some on chemisms and tropisms. They also have their systems of communication—though we are inclined to assume that these are "egocentric" ones. The achievement of abstraction necessary to formulate the "No" raises communication to the allocentric level. With this it becomes the matrix of social relations on the human level.

Looking back on our findings about the origin of communication, it has become clear that at birth, and for a long time afterwards, action and communication are one. Action,

NO AND YES

performed by the neonate, is only discharge of drive. But the same action, when viewed by the observer, contains a message from the neonate.

Communication became segregated from action through the repetitive experiences of delay in need gratification. This frustration transforms action, which is a path of discharge, into an avenue of communication. A long process of development—long in terms of the infant's life—leads to the point where action and communication clearly separate from each other. Then communication becomes directed; still later communication evolves into a suitable substitute for action in social intercourse, when the toddler becomes aware that he is directing a message to the "other." Symbols, gestural or verbal, are now used to convey not only ideational contents, but also mental operations in the nature of dynamic processes. The earliest representatives of abstractive symbol gestures are the head-shaking "No" and the head-nodding "Yes."

But we must not overlook that while the *semantic* gesture of head-nodding assent has the diametrically opposite meaning of head-shaking refusal, this antithesis is nonexistent in the motor prototypes of the two gestures. Both head-shaking rooting as well as head-nodding movements toward the breast are provoked by the unpleasure arising in states of inner tension. Head-shaking and head-nodding are both the expression of an appetitive, assenting, affirmative endeavor— in Freud's terms, of a striving toward union; in one word: of a "Yes."

For the unconscious does not have a "No." Therefore, the motor prototypes of "Yes" and "No," the first form in which these gestures arose in the neonate who lacks consciousness, was "Yes."

Psychoanalytically this is evident. But it is equally stringent for the tenets of developmental psychology. Developmentally the two gesture prototypes arise in the period of nondiffer-entiation, when not only "Yes" was undistinguishable from "No," but when even crying is confused with laughing by the observer.

Differentiation of these manifestations, as of every other sector of the infant's personality, must take place before even the first stage of directed presemantic communication can appear. But differentiation is a progressive process which unfolds in the framework of object relations. Each of the successive steps of this process is marked by the creation of a growing body of behavior patterns aiming at communica-tion. One after the other of these patterns is abandoned because they no longer are suitable to express the increasing complexity of that which the child wishes to communicate. Besides creating new behavior patterns like vocalization, etc., the child also has recourse to already abandoned ones. Among these head-nodding and head-shaking are particu-larly suitable, because of their derivation from the original approach behavior to the consummation of need gratifica-tion. They will become the eventual representatives of re-fusal and assent and at the same time the first indicators of abstractive ideational processes.

Head-shaking and head-nodding are superior for the pur-poses of communication to other motor behaviors for an-other reason also. They are the most conspicuous and con-sistent behavior patterns of the frustrating love object. The child obtains them through the mechanism of identification with the aggressor. This is the process by which the phylo-genetically available motor pattern is pressed eventually into service as the ontogenetically developed gesture of semantic communication.

We have tried to present some factual data and the tenta-tive ideas we have of this process. Our best knowledge of it is contained in Freud's "Negation." It will be the task of future research to unravel the successive steps in this process through further observation.

In summing up the conclusions at which we have arrived, we will begin by stating that archaic motor patterns are used in conveying the concepts of "No" and "Yes" by gesture. These motor patterns are part of the Anlage and available already at birth. Phylogenetically speaking, the morphological structures necessary for the performance of these movements are present in man as in all mammals. Beyond this morphological potential we found that head-shaking, in the form of cephalogyric movements, is a firmly established mammalian behavior pattern handed down through phylogenesis in altricials.

Head-nodding also has an evolutionary history which goes back to the ethological class of precocials. In man both motor patterns can be demonstrated in the nursing situation, suggesting that man combines certain attributes of the altricials with some of the attributes of the precocials. But while head rotation in man in response to tactile stimulation is already present at birth, head-nodding is not. Head-nodding in man will be activated only when at three months he achieves that stage of maturity which the precocial possesses already at birth.

The role of these two motor patterns in earliest oral need gratification makes them suitable for eventual use as a device of communication.

However, the fact that the motor pattern of head-shaking is phylogenetically inherited, is in itself not enough to determine its use for communication. Even the additional fact that it ensures survival in the need-gratificatory processes of earliest nutrition is insufficient to endow it with the meaning it will ultimately have as a semantic signal, although it does contribute to this meaning.

Both the motor pattern and the need-gratificatory function are the product of inherited maturational processes. The attribution of semantic meaning to the motor pattern, however, is brought about by a developmental process, by interchanges in the framework of object relations. Semantic gesture and word can only be evolved when the interaction between object relations and endopsychic energy displacements forces a specific change in the structure of the ego. The realignment in the ego takes the form of the defense mechanism of identification with the aggressor.

Therefore the semantic use of head-shaking "No" and head-nodding "Yes" is predicated on the individual personal history. But in the first year of life personal history is largely determined by two conditions which apply universally to mankind: they are the infant's helplessness on the one hand, and the mother's urge to provide for his every need on the other. The appearance of the cephalogyric motor pattern at birth is the phylogenetic precipitate, a vector, as it were, of these two forces. They continue to interact throughout the first year of life and together with cephalogyric motions and other congenital equipment are the givens of object relations.

Accordingly, though by no means ubiquitous, head-shaking "No" and head-nodding "Yes" belong probably to the most widespread semantic gestures on the globe. The fact that a number of cultures may exist (and actually do exist) in which head-nodding means "No," others where head-shaking means "Yes," and still others where the two may be unknown, does not invalidate our thesis. Our argument has shown, we believe, that these alternates will prove to have their origin in peculiarities of the child-rearing practices, of the institutions and of the history of the culture in question.

The existence of such deviant semantic gestures does not affect our assumptions regarding the manner in which the earliest semantic gestures are acquired. Furthermore, it has no bearing on our proposition concerning the dynamics which result in the first concept formation. These include the use of aggressive cathexis for mental operations and the attachment of aggressive charges to a device used in object relations, *resulting in the replacement of action, destructive or otherwise, by communication*. This formulation holds equally true in those cultures which do not use the head-shaking "No" or the head-nodding "Yes."

The use of head-shaking and head-nodding as semantic signals is widespread but not universal. What is universal is the road that leads to their development, even if the gesture which eventually emerges is different. Starting with the inborn motor pattern of rooting in the neonate, who is not conscious and for whom the "No" is nonexistent, this road leads ultimately to the concept of negation and to the conscious use of the semantic "No" for communication. This is the road to the humanization of man.

Bibliography

ADATTO, C. P. (1956), On Pouting. *J. Am. Psa. Assn.*, V.

ADRIAN, E. D. (1946), The Mental and the Physical Origins of Behavior. *Int. J. Psa.*, XXVII.

BAERENDS, G. P. (1950), Specializations in Organs and Movements with a Releasing Function. *Sympos. Soc. Exper. Biol.*, IV.

BALDWIN, A. C. (1955), *Behavior and Development in Children.* New York: Dryden.

BERNFELD, S. (1925), *Psychologie des Säuglings.* Vienna: Springer.

BIERENS DE HAAN, J. A. (1929), Animal Language in Its Relation to That of Man. *Proceedings of the Cambridge Philosophical Society.* Cambridge: University Press.

BOLK, L. (1926), *Das Problem der Menschwerdung.* Jena: Fischer.

BOWLBY, J. (1953), Critical Phases in the Development of Social Responses in Man. *New Biology*, XIV. London: Penguin Books.

BRODY, S. (1956), *Patterns of Mothering.* New York: International Universities Press.

BUEHLER, K. (1924), *Die geistige Entwicklung des Kindes.* Jena: Gustav Fischer.

—— (1934), *Sprachtheorie.* Jena: Gustav Fischer.

BYCHOWSKI, G. (1956), The Ego and the Introjects. *Psa. Quart.*, XXV.

CARMICHAEL, L. (1934), An Experimental Study in the Prenatal Guinea Pig of the Origin and Development of Reflexes and Patterns of Behavior in Relation to the Stimulation of Specific Receptor Areas during the Period of Active Fetal Life. *Genet. Psychol. Mon.*, XVI.

CHRISTOFFEL, H. (1950), Gähnen und sich Dehnen (Räkeln) [yawning and stretching]. *Schweiz. med. Wschr.*, LXXXI.

COBLINER, W. G. (1955), Intracommunication and Attitude: A Methodological Note. *J. Psychol.*, XXXIX.

CRAIG, W. (1922), A Note on Darwin's Work "The Expression of the Emotions in Man and Animals." *J. Abn. & Soc. Psychol.*, XVI.

CRITCHLEY, M. (1939), *The Language of Gesture*. London: E. Arnold & Co.

DARWIN, C. R. (1873), *The Expression of the Emotions in Man and Animals*. New York: Philosophical Library, 1955.

—— (1877), A Biographical Sketch of an Infant. *Mind*, II.

DEARBORN, G. V. N. (1910), *Motor Sensory Development. Observations on the First Three Years of a Child*. Baltimore: Warwick & York.

DE LAGUNA, G. M. (1927), *Speech, Its Function and Development*. New Haven: Yale Univ. Press.

DEUTSCH, F. (1947), Analysis of Postural Behavior. *Psa. Quart.*, XVI.

—— (1949), Thus Speaks the Body. *Transactions of the N. Y. Academy of Sciences*, Series 2, XII, No. 2.

—— (1952), Analytic Posturology. *Psa. Quart.*, XXI.

DONALDSON, H. H. (1916), Growth Changes in the Mammalian Nervous System. *Harvey Lecture Series*, XII.

ENGEL, G. L. & REICHSMAN, F. (1956), Spontaneous and Experimentally Induced Depression in an Infant with a Gastric Fistula: A Contribution to the Problem of Depression. *J. Am. Psa. Assn.*, IV.

FABER (1850), Über das krampfhafte Kopfnicken. *J. f. Kinderkrankheiten* (Erlangen), XIV.

FENICHEL, O. (1945), *The Psychoanalytic Theory of Neurosis*. New York: W. W. Norton.

FINKELSTEIN, H. (1938), *Säuglingskrankheiten*. Amsterdam: Elsevier.

FLACH, A. (1928), Psychologie der Ausdrucksbewegungen. *Arch. d. ges. Psychol.*, LXV.

FLUGEL, J. C. (1930), *The Psychology of Clothes*. London: Hogarth.

FOULKES (FUCHS), S. H. (1937), On Introjection. *Int. J. Psa.*, XVIII.

FREUD, A. (1936), *The Ego and the Mechanisms of Defense*. New York: International Universities Press, 1946.

—— (1951), A Connection between the States of Negativism and of Emotional Surrender. Paper read at the 17th Int. Psa. Congress. Abstract: *Int. J. Psa.*, XXXIII, 1952.

—— (1952), The Role of Bodily Illness in the Mental Life of Children. *The Psychoanalytic Study of the Child*, VII. New York: International Universities Press.

—— (1953), Some Remarks on Infant Observation. *The Psychoanalytic Study of the Child*, VIII. New York: International Universities Press.

FREUD, S. (1895), Entwurf einer Psychologie. In: *Aus den Anfängen der Psychoanalyse*. London: Imago Publ. Co., 1950.

—— (1895a), Project for a Scientific Psychology. In: *The Origins of Psychoanalysis.* New York: Basic Books, 1954.

—— (1900), The Interpretation of Dreams. *Standard Edition,* III & IV. London: Hogarth Press, 1953.

—— (1905), Fragment of an Analysis of a Case of Hysteria. *Standard Edition,* VII. London: Hogarth Press, 1953.

—— (1905a), Three Essays on the Theory of Sexuality. *Standard Edition,* VII. London: Hogarth Press, 1953.

—— (1905b), Wit and Its Relation to the Unconscious. *The Basic Writings of Sigmund Freud.* New York: Random House, 1938.

—— (1908), Character and Anal Erotism. *Collected Papers,* II. London: Hogarth Press, 1924.

—— (1910), The Antithetical Meaning of Primal Words. *Collected Papers,* IV. London: Hogarth Press, 1925.

—— (1911), Formulations Regarding the Two Principles in Mental Functioning. *Collected Papers,* IV. London: Hogarth Press, 1925.

—— (1914), On Narcissism: An Introduction. *Collected Papers,* IV. London: Hogarth Press, 1925.

—— (1917), *A General Introduction to Psychoanalysis.* Garden City, N. Y.: Garden City Publishing Co., 1943.

—— (1920), Beyond the Pleasure Principle. *Standard Edition,* XVIII. London: Hogarth Press, 1955.

—— (1924), Metapsychological Supplement to the Theory of Dreams. *Collected Papers,* IV. London: Hogarth Press, 1925.

—— (1925), Negation. *Collected Papers,* V. London: Hogarth Press, 1950.

—— (1926), *The Problem of Anxiety.* New York: W. W. Norton, 1936.

—— (1931), Female Sexuality. *Collected Papers,* V. London: Hogarth Press, 1950.

—— (1938), Splitting of the Ego in the Defensive Process. *Collected Papers,* V. London: Hogarth Press, 1950.

—— (1939), *An Outline of Psychoanalysis.* New York: W. W. Norton, 1949.

FRIES, M. (1947), Diagnosing the Child's Adjustment through Age-Level Tests. *Psa. Rev.,* XXXIV.

GAMPER, E. (1926), Bau und Leistung eines menschlichen Mittelhirnwesens, II. *Ztschr. f. d. ges. Neurol. & Psychiat.,* CIV.

GARDNER, G. E. (1956), Affects, Object Relations and Gastric Secretions. Panel Report. Annual Meeting, Am. Psa. Assn., 1955. *J. Am. Psa. Assn.,* IV.

GESELL, A. (1954), The Ontogenesis of Infant Behavior. In: *Manual of Child Psychology,* ed. L. Carmichael. 2nd Ed. New York: J. Wiley & Sons.

GLAUBER, I. P. (1943), Psychoanalytic Concepts of the Stutterer. *Nerv. Child,* II.

GLOVER, E. (1930), Grades of Ego-Differentiation. In: *On the Early Development of Mind.* New York: International Universities Press, 1956.

—— (1933), The Relation of Perversion Formation to the Development of the Reality Sense. *Int. J. Psa.,* XIV.

—— (1935), The Developmental Study of the Obsessional Neurosis. *Int. J. Psa.,* XVI.

—— (1943), The Concept of Dissociation. In: *On the Early Development of Mind.* New York: International Universities Press, 1956.

GOSTYNSKI, E. (1951), A Clinical Contribution to the Analysis of Gestures. *Int. J. Psa.,* XXXII.

GREENSON, R. R. (1949), The Psychology of Apathy. *Psa. Quart.,* XVIII.

—— (1954), The Struggle against Identification. *J. Am. Psa. Assn.,* II.

—— (1954), About the Sound "Mm . . ." *Psa. Quart.,* XXIII.

GUNTHER, M. (1956), Instincts and the Nursing Couple. *Lancet,* CCLXVIII.

HARTMANN, H. (1939), Ichpsychologie und Anpassungsproblem. *Int. Ztschr. f. Psa. & Imago,* XXIV. Transl. in part in: *Organization and Pathology of Thought,* ed. D. Rapaport. New York: Columbia University Press, 1951.

—— (1947), On Rational and Irrational Action. In: *Psychoanalysis and the Social Sciences,* I. New York: International Universities Press.

—— (1950), Comments on the Psychoanalytic Theory of the Ego. *The Psychoanalytic Study of the Child,* V. New York: International Universities Press.

—— (1951), Technical Implications of Ego Psychology. *Psa. Quart.,* XX.

—— (1953), Contribution to the Metapsychology of Schizophrenia. *The Psychoanalytic Study of the Child,* VIII. New York: International Universities Press.

—— (1955), Notes on the Theory of Sublimation. *The Psychoanalytic Study of the Child,* X. New York: International Universities Press.

—— (1956), The Development of the Ego Concept in Freud's Work. *Int. J. Psa.,* XXXVII.

—— & KRIS, E., LOEWENSTEIN, R. M. (1946), Comments on the Formation of Psychic Structure. *The Psychoanalytic Study of the Child,* II. New York: International Universities Press.

HEBB, D. O. (1955), The Mammal and His Environment. *Am. J. Psychiat.,* CXI.

HOFFER, W. (1949), Mouth, Hand and Ego Integration. *The Psychoanalytic Study of the Child,* III/IV. New York: International Universities Press.

—— (1950), Oral Aggressiveness and Ego Development. *Int. J. Psa.*, XXXI.

HOOKER, D. (1939), Fetal Behavior. *Publ. Assn. Res. Nerv. & Ment. Dis.*, XIX.

—— (1952), *The Prenatal Origin of Behavior.* Lawrence: Univ. of Kansas Press.

HOWE, L. P. (1955), Some Sociological Aspects of Identification. In: *Psychoanalysis and the Social Sciences,* IV. New York: International Universities Press.

HUG-HELLMUTH, H. (1919), A Study of the Mental Life of the Child. *Nerv. & Ment. Dis. Monogr.,* XXIX.

—— (1921), *Aus dem Seelenleben des Kindes.* Leipzig-Vienna: Deuticke.

INHELDER, B. (1956), Die affektive und kognitive Entwicklung des Kindes. *Schweiz. Ztschr. f. Psychol.,* XV.

ISAKOWER, O. (1938), A Contribution to the Pathopsychology of Phenomena Associated with Falling Asleep. *Int. J. Psa.,* XIX.

JACOBSON, E. (1954), The Self and the Object World. *The Psychoanalytic Study of the Child,* IX. New York: International Universities Press.

JAMES, W. (1890), *Principles of Psychology.* New York: Dover Publications, 1950.

KASANIN, J. S. (1944), *Language and Thought in Schizophrenia.* Berkeley: University of California Press.

KRIS, E. (1950), *Psychoanalytic Explorations in Art.* New York: International Universities Press.

—— (1955), Neutralization and Sublimation: Observations on Young Children. *The Psychoanalytic Study of the Child,* X. New York: International Universities Press.

—— (1956), On Some Vicissitudes of Insight in Psychoanalysis. *Int. J. Psa.,* XXXVII.

—— & SPEIER, H., et al. (1944), *German Radio Propaganda. Report on Home Broadcasts During the War.* London, New York: Oxford University Press.

KROUT, M. (1935), Autistic Gestures. *Psychol. Monogr.,* CCVIII.

KUBIE, L. S. (1953), The Distortion of the Symbolic Process in Neurosis and Psychosis. *J. Am. Psa. Assn.,* I.

—— (1956), Influence of Symbolic Processes on the Role of Instincts in Human Behavior. *Psychosom. Med.,* XVIII.

KULOVESI, Y. (1939), Die Ausdrucksbewegungen der Bejahung und der Verneinung. *Int. Ztschr. f. Psa.,* XXIV.

KUSSMAUL, A. (1859), *Untersuchungen über das Seelenleben des neugeborenen Menschen.* Leipzig: Winter.

[155]

LA BARRE, W. (1947), The Cultural Basis of Emotions and Gestures. *J. of Personality*, XVI.

LALANDE, A. (1932), *Vocabulaire de la philosophie*. Paris: Alcan.

LANDAUER, K. (1926), Die kindliche Bewegungsunruhe. *Int. Ztschr. f. Psa.*, XII.

LATIF, I. (1934), The Physiological Basis of Linguistic Development and of the Ontogeny of Meaning, I, II, III. *Psychol. Rev.*, XLI.

LEVY, D. M. (1934), Experiments on the Sucking Reflex and Social Behavior of Dogs. *Am. J. Orthopsychiat.*, IV.

LEWIN, B. D. (1946), Sleep, the Mouth and the Dream Screen. *Psa. Quart.*, XV.

—— (1950), *The Psychoanalysis of Elation*. New York: W. W. Norton.

—— (1953), The Forgetting of Dreams. In: *Drives, Affects, Behavior*, ed. R. M. Loewenstein. New York: International Universities Press.

LEWIS, M. M. (1936), *Infant Speech*. London: Kegan Paul.

LINN, L. (1955), A Psychoanalytic Contribution to Comparative Neuropsychiatry. Paper read at the Midwinter Meeting of the American Psychoanalytic Association, New York, December 1955.

LOEWENSTEIN, R. M. (1956), Some Remarks on the Role of Speech in Psycho-Analysis. *Int. J. Psa.*, XXXVII.

LORENZ, K. (1950), The Comparative Method in Studying Innate Behavior Patterns. *Sympos. Soc. Exper. Biol.* IV.

MAGNUS, R. (1924), *Körperstellung*. Berlin: Springer.

—— & DE KLEYN, A. (1912), Die Abhängigkeit des Tonus der Extremitätsmuskeln von der Kopfstellung. *Pflüg. Arch. ges. Physiol.*, CXLV.

MAHLER, M. S. (1952), On Child Psychosis and Schizophrenia: Autistic and Symbiotic Infantile Psychoses. *The Psychoanalytic Study of the Child*, VII. New York: International Universities Press.

—— & GOSLINER, B. J. (1955), On Symbiotic Child Psychosis. *The Psychoanalytic Study of the Child*, X. New York: International Universities Press.

MARGOLIN, S. G. (1953), Psychophysiological Studies of Fistulous Openings into the Gastrointestinal Tract. *J. Mt. Sinai Hosp.*, XX.

—— (1953a), Genetic and Dynamic Psychophysiological Determinants of Pathophysiological Processes. In: *The Psychosomatic Concept in Psychoanalysis*, ed. F. Deutsch. New York: International Universities Press.

—— (1954), Psychotherapeutic Principles in Psychosomatic Practice. In: *Recent Developments in Psychosomatic Medicine*, ed. E. D. Wittkower and R. A. Cleghorn. Philadelphia: J. B. Lippincott.

MASSERMAN, J. H. (1944), Language, Behavior and Dynamic Psychiatry. *Int. J. Psa.*, XXV.

McGraw, M. B. (1935), *Growth: A Study of Johnny and Jimmy*. New York: Appleton-Century.

—— (1946), Maturation of Behavior. In: *Manual of Child Psychology*, ed. L. Carmichael. New York: J. Wiley & Sons.

Mead, G. H. (1934), *Mind, Self, and Society*. Chicago: Univ. of Chicago Press.

Meerloo, J. A. M. (1952), *Conversation and Communication*. New York: International Universities Press.

Minkowski, M. (1916), Zur Physiologie der vorderen und hinteren Zentralwindung. Paper read at the XI. Meeting of the Schweiz. Neurol. Gesellschaft, Bern, May 13-14th. *Neurol. Centralblatt*, XXXVI, 1917.

—— (1922), Über frühzeitige Bewegungen und muskuläre Reaktionen beim menschlichen Foetus und ihre Beziehungen zum foetalen Nerven- und Muskelsystem. *Schweiz. med. Wschr.*, III.

Mittelmann, B. (1954), Motility in Infants, Children and Adults. *The Psychoanalytic Study of the Child*, IX. New York: International Universities Press.

Montagu, M. F. A. (1950), Constitutional and Prenatal Factors in Infant and Child Health. *Problems of Infancy and Childhood*. New York: Josiah Macy Jr. Foundation.

—— (1953), The Sensory Influences of the Skin. *Texas Reports on Biol. & Med.*, XI.

Nunberg, H. (1931), The Synthetic Function of the Ego. In: *Practice and Theory of Psychoanalysis*. New York: International Universities Press, 1955.

—— (1952), Panel on Problem of Identification. Reporter: H. A. Wiggers. Midwinter Meeting 1952. *J. Am. Psa. Assn.*, I. (p. 547).

Ostow, M. (1955), Psychic Contents and Processes of the Brain. *Psychosom. Med.*, XVII.

Pepys, S. (1667), *Diary*.

Piaget, J. (1936), *The Origins of Intelligence in Children*. New York: International Universities Press, 1952.

—— (1945), *Play, Dreams and Imitation in Childhood*. New York: W. W. Norton, 1951.

Ploss, H., Bartels, M. & Bartels, P. (1927), *Das Weib*. Berlin: Neufeld & Henius Verlag.

Portmann, A. (1951), *Biologische Fragmente zu einer Lehre vom Menschen*, Basel: B. Schwabe & Co.

—— (1953), *Das Tier als soziales Wesen*. Zürich: Rhein Verlag.

—— (1956), *Zoologie und das neue Bild des Menschen*. Hamburg: Rowohlt.

[157]

PRATT, K. C. (1946), The Neonate. In: *Manual of Child Psychology,* ed. L. Carmichael. New York: J. Wiley & Sons, Inc.

PRECHTL, H. F. R. (1950, 1951), Auslösende und steuernde Mechanismen des Saugaktes. *Ztschr. vergl. Physiol.* XXXII, XXXIII.

—— (1952), Angeborene Bewegungsweisen junger Katzen. *Experientia,* VIII.

—— (1952a), Über die Adaptation des angeborenen Auslösemechanismus. *Die Naturwissenschaften.* XXXIX.

—— (1955), *Die Entwicklung der frühkindlichen Motorik I, II, III.* A motion picture. Institut für den wissenschaftlichen Film. Goettingen.

—— & SCHLEIDT, W. M. (1950), *Ztschr. f. vgl. Physiol.,* XXXII.

PREYER, W. (1893), *Mental Development in the Child.* New York: Appleton.

RANGELL, L. (1954), The Psychology of Poise. *Int. J. Psa.,* XXXV.

RAPAPORT, D. (1950), Book Review of N. Wiener's *Cybernetics. Psa. Quart.,* XIX.

—— (1951), Toward a Theory of Thinking. In: *Organization and Pathology of Thought.* New York: Columbia University Press.

RAUDNITZ, R. W. (1897), Zur Lehre vom Spasmus Nutans. *J. f. Kinderh.,* Leipzig, XLV.

REVESZ, G. (1956), *The Origins and Prehistory of Language.* New York: Philosophical Library.

RIPPIN, R. & HETZER, H. (1930), Frühestes Lernen des Säuglings in der Ernährungssituation. *Ztschr. f. Psychol.* CXVIII.

RUSSELL, B. (1948), *Human Knowledge, Its Scope and Limits.* New York: Simon & Schuster.

SCHILDER, P. (1935), *The Image and Appearance of the Human Body.* New York: International Universities Press, 1950.

SCOTT, J. P. & MARSTON, M. V. (1950), Critical Periods Affecting the Development of Normal and Mal-Adjustive Social Behavior of Puppies. *J. Genet. Psychol.,* LXXVII.

SEITZ, A. (1940), Die Paarbildung bei einigen Cichliden I. *Ztschr. f. Tierpsychol.,* IV.

SHARPE, E. F. (1940), Psychophysical Problems Revealed in Language: An Examination of Metaphor. *Int. J. Psa.* XXI.

SHERRINGTON, C. S. (1906), *The Integrative Action of the Nervous System.* New Haven: Yale University Press. 1947.

SPIELREIN, S. (1922), Die Entstehung der kindlichen Worte Papa und Mama. *Imago.* VIII.

SPITZ, R. A. (1934), Points cruciaux du développement psychique de l'enfant. Lecture given at the Sorbonne.

—— (1945), Diacritic and Coenesthetic Organizations. *Psa. Rev.,* XXXII.

—— (1945a), Hospitalism. *The Psychoanalytic Study of the Child*. I. New York: International Universities Press.

—— (1947), *Weaning*. A motion picture. Studies of the Psychoanalytic Research Project on Problems of Infancy (not released).

—— (1950), Anxiety in Infancy: A Study of Its Manifestations in the First Year of Life. *Int. J. Psa.*, XXXI.

—— (1951), Purposive Grasping. *J. Personal.*, I.

—— (1954), Genèse des premières relations objectales. *Rev. Franç. Psychanal.*, XVIII.

—— (1954a), Infantile Depression and the General Adaptation Syndrome. In: *Depression*, ed. P. H. Hoch & J. Zubin. New York: Grune & Stratton.

—— (1955), A Note on the Extrapolation of Ethological Findings. *Int. J. Psa.*, XXXVI.

—— (1955a), The Primal Cavity. *The Psychoanalytic Study of the Child*, X. New York: International Universities Press.

—— (1957), *Die Entstehung der ersten Objektbeziehungen*. Stuttgart: Klett.

STERBA, R. (1934), The Fate of the Ego in Analytic Therapy. *Int. J. Psa.*, XV.

SUGAR, N. (1941), Zur Frage der mimischen Bejahung und Verneinung. *Int. Ztschr. Psa.*, XXVI.

TAINE, H. (1876), Note sur l'acquisition du langage chez les enfants et dans l'espèce humaine. *Rev. Phil.*, I. Transl. in: *Mind*, II, 1877.

TILNEY, F. & CASAMAJOR, L. (1924), Myelinogeny as Applied to the Study of Behavior. *Arch. Neurol. & Psychiat.*, XII.

—— & KUBIE, L. S. (1931), Behavior and Its Relation to the Development of the Brain. *Bull. Neurol. Inst. of N.Y.*, I.

TINBERGEN, N. (1951), *The Study of Instincts*. London: Oxford University Press.

VON SENDEN, M. (1932), *Raum und Gestaltauffassung bei operierten Blindgeborenen vor und nach der Operation*. Leipzig: Johann Ambrosius Barth.

WARREN, H. (1935), *Dictionary of Psychology*. Boston: Houghton, Mifflin.

WATSON, J. B. (1924), *Behaviorism*. New York: W. W. Norton.

ZAPPERT, J. (1924), Zur Lehre vom Spasmus Nutans. *Med. Klin. Berlin*, XX.

ZEIGARNIK, B. (1927), Über das Behalten von erledigten und unerledigten Handlungen. *Psychol. Forsch.*, IX.

Index

Abel, K., 95
Abstraction, 44, 52, 56-59, 99-102, 104, 130, 145
Action
  and communication, 26, 131-132, 145-150
  delay of, 25-27, 145-149
Activity
  pattern, 107
  shift from passivity to, 45-48, 53-57, 134, 137
Adaptation, 23-26, 40, 45-56, 91
Adatto, C. P., 67, 151
Adrian, E. D., 151
Adultomorphic interpretation, 37
Affect, 49-51
  deprivation, 135; see also Child, deprived
  inappropriate, 140-141
  see also Emotion
Affirmation, 34, 98, 103-116, 146-149
Age (references to developmental phases)
  3 months, 50, 90, 101, 108-109, 112-114, 119, 122, 136, 140
  6 months, 40, 94
  8 months, 53-54, 94, 120, 127; see also Anxiety, eight-months
  15-18 months, 39, 46, 49-50, 67, 95, 101, 103, 119, 123, 128-130, 140, 144
Aggression
  and "No," 47, 51-52, 56-59, 130-133

and object relations, ix, 130-133
and thought processes, 58, 130, 150
Altricials, 23-31, 70, 111-112, 148
Ambivalence, 55, 96
Amnesia, infantile, 41
Anaclitic situation, 74, 83-85, 102
Anaclitic therapy, 126
Anal phase, 139-141; see also Stubbornness
Anencephalic monster, 21, 70
Animals, 92, 141, 145, 148
  language of, 7
  nursing behavior of, 22-23, 111-112
  rooting behavior in, 19, 22
Anxiety
  eight-months (of stranger), 13, 53-55, 72-73, 76-77, 101, 122, 142-144
  in infancy, ix
Apperception, 116
Appetitive behavior, 34, 65, 104
Approach behavior, 89-90, 95, 98, 108-110, 147
Aristotle, 104
Atresia esophagi, congenital, 17, 71-85
Autoerotism, ix, 10
Autonomy, secondary, 37
Autism, 140-141
Avoidance, 17-19, 76, 93-95, 98-99; see also Child, refusal of contact; Perception
Awareness, emergence of, 114-150

[161]

Communication *(cont'd)*
  psychoanalytic studies of, 3-6
  semantic, 131-136
  verbal, 139-150
Concentration camp, 64
Concept formation, 39, 52-53, 99-102;
  see also Abstraction, Thought
  processes
Consciousness, 90, 104; *see also*
  Awareness
Consummatory behavior, 65, 89-91,
  109-110, 147
Contact perception, 28-30
Countertransference, 61
Craig, W., 152
"Crawling approach reaction," 31
Critchley, M., 152
Culture, as "secondary nature of
  man," 23
Cup-feeding, 94-95
Curiosity, 133

Darwin, C. R., 19, 152
Day residue, 79
Dearborn, G. V. N., 152
Death, 75, 80
Defense
  anaclitic, 76
  prestage of, 55
  prototype of, 76
  see also Identification with the aggressor, Regression, Repression
de Kleyn, 21
De Laguna, G. M., 152
Denial, 18, 55, 89
Dereism, 141
Detour behavior, 26, 65-66, 91, 145
Deutsch, F., 3, 152
Development
  and maturation, imbalance between, 142-144
  critical (crucial) stages, 82, 141;
  see also Organizers
  law of, 48
  objectless stage, 66, 126
  specific age references, *see* Age
  stages of, 34-35, 89-102, 120-150
Dewey, J., 71

Diacritic perception (discrimination), 50, 77, 112
Discharge
  pathways of, 4-5, 86
  primary and secondary function, 6-
  7, 86
  see also Tension
Discrimination, 51-52, 101; *see also*
  Diacritic perception, Judgment,
  Perception
Dissociation
  and splitting, 141
  law of, 44
Dogs, 134-135
Donaldson, H. H., 152
Dream, xi, 18, 74, 87, 139
  forgetting of, 78-80
  screen, 77-79, 114
Drives
  aim of, 91
  anaclitic unfolding of, 83-84
  and intellect, 86-89
  attribute of, 34, 104-106

Ego
  acquisition of negation, 53; *see also*
  "No"
  and adaptation, 23, 118
  and "egocentric," 7
  and "I," 115, 120-122
  and identification, 43, 52, 149
  and judgment, 87-88, 101
  and memory, 94
  and self, 115-150
  apparatus, 39, 129
  as observer, 133
  ideal, 122
  in deprived children, 40
  in pathological conditions, 96
  narcissististic stage, 45
  nuclei, 91
  ontogenesis of, ix, 94-96
  organizing (integrative) function,
  118
  splitting of, 140-141
  synthetic activity of, 57, 118
  syntonicity, 79
  undifferentiated phase, 39

[163]

Embryology, 70, 142
Emotion, pure, 78; *see also* **Affect**
Empathy, 50
Engel, G. L., xi, 17, 71-73, 83, 152
Energy, transformation of, 52
Erotogenic zones, 83-84; *see also* **Oral zone**
Ethology, 15, 22, 29-30, 33, 81-83
Evolution
  and delay of action, 25-27, 147-149
  and principle of parsimony, 25
  see also Behavior, **Ontogenesis, Phylogenesis**

Faber, 12, 152
Face
  and nursing, 32-33, 112-115
  and object relations, 75-76, 81; *see also* Primal cavity
Facial mimetic behavior, 67-68
Fantasy, regressive, 67-68
Feces, 140
Feeding
  behavior of animals, 19, 22
  dissociated from mouth, *see* Atresia esophagi
  impact of different techniques, 85
  interruption of, 108-109
  see also Breast-feeding, Cup-feeding, Nursing, Oral phase, Rooting
Femininity, 137
Fenichel, O., 91, 152
Fetal behavior, 20, 32
Finkelstein, H., 12, 152
Fixation
  and organizers, 83, 143
  and regression, 81
Flach, A., 152
Flight reaction, 17-18
Flugel, J. C., 152
Folklore, 87
Foulkes (Fuchs), S. H., 152
Freud, Anna, 45-48, 55, 100, 118-119, 124, 129, 133, 137, 140, 152
Freud, Sigmund, x *et passim.*
  bibliographical references to, 152-153

on active mastery of passive experience, 45-47
on beginning of communication, 4-5, 86-88
on drives, 83, 105
on ego development, 124
on judgment, 54, 90-91
on mimicry, 39
on negation, 86-91, 102, 106, 148
on origin of communication, 39, 86-88
on primal words, 95
on reality testing, 92
on repression, 86-89
on self-regard, 121-122
on splitting of ego, 141
on symbol, 87
on tension discharge, 4-5, 86-88
on thought processes, 25-26, 87-88, 91-92
on unconscious, 90, 105
"Project for a Scientific Psychology," 4-5, 87-88
Fries, M., 107, 153
Frontal lobe lesions, 16
Frustration
  affective, 58
  and aggressive cathexis, 45-47, 56-59, 130-133
  and establishment of self, 136-141
  and hallucinatory gratification, 18-19
  and prohibition, 44-49, 56, 127, 146
  and regression, 18-19, 67
  of frustrator, 132
Function, *see* Change of function

Games, 42, 129-130
Gamper, E., 21-22, 27, 29, 32, 62, 153
Gardner, G. E., 153
Gaskill, H., x
Gastric fistula, 71-85
Gesell, A., 19, 153
Gestalt psychology, 44
Gesture, semantic; *see* Head-nodding, Head-shaking, Identification
Glauber, I. P., 154

Glover, E., 34, 91, 104, 119, 141, 143, 154
Goldstein, K., 135
Gosliner, B. J., 156
Gostynski, E., 154
Grasping
  (hand, fingers), 16, 22, 62, 114-115
  oral, 22
Gratification, and regression, 80-81; *see also* Frustration, Hallucinatory gratification, Need gratification
Greenson, R. R., 3, 154
Gunther, M., 154

Hallucinatory gratification, 77-80, 110, 138-139
Hand
  and refusal gesture, 72-76
  -mouth coordination, 21, 32, 63
  movements and nursing, 114-115
Hartmann, H., 23, 37, 39, 117-119, 122, 127, 130, 133, 136, 140, 154
Head
  -banging, 10, 13
  -nodding "Yes," 103-116, 146-150
  -rolling (rotation), 9-13, 20-22, 36-37, 98, 101
  -shaking "No," 9, 13, 16-17, 34-59, 67-68, 73-75, 82, 85, 94-108, 146-150
Hebb, D. O., 134-135, 154
Heidegger, M., 104
Hetzer, H., 19, 107, 158
Hoch, P. H., 159
Hoffer, W., 21, 154-155
Hooker, D., 20, 155
Hospitalism, 9-11, 34, 36, 83; *see also* Child, deprived
Howe, L. P., 47, 155
Hug-Hellmuth, H., 3-4, 155
Humor, 42, 98
Hunger, 37, 91

"I," and "non-I," 40, 113-116, 120, 127, 136, 144

Identification
  and semantic meaning, 38-59, 96, 98-99
  of parents with child, 41-42, 98-99
  primary, 40
  reciprocal, 98-99
  selectivity in, 49-52
  with aggressor, 46-49, 51-52, 55-57, 67, 96, 122, 127-130, 132-133, 147-149
  with frustrator, 46, 56
  with gesture, 40-43, 54-59
Imitation, 14, 99
  and identification, 40-43, 48, 52
Inanimate object, 122, 144
Indicators of psychic organizers, 142-150
Infant
  dependence (helplessness) of, 5, 23, 83-85, 149
  frustration tolerance, 107-109
  motion pictures of, 20-21, 71-72, 107-110, 138
  nature of communication in, 5-7
  normal, 13, 35, 39, 74
  nursing behavior of, 19-22, 28, 32-33, 67-69, 93-95, 97-98, 108-116
  premature, 35
  signs of unpleasure in, 10-11, 16, 75, 90
  with congenital atresia esophagi, 17, 71-85
  without brain, 21
  see also Child, Neonate
Inhelder, B., 58, 155
Innate releasing mechanism (IRM)
  and rooting, 33, 70, 81-83
  definition of, 30
Instincts
  and adaptation, 23
  attribute of, 104-105
  see also Drives, Need gratification
Interpersonal, 71
Intracommunication, 47
Intrapersonal, 71
Intrasystemic relations, 118, 140
Isakower, O., 21, 155
Isolation, 58

Mother *(cont'd)*
unconscious response to infant's signals, 64
Motor patterns, early, 13-17, 63, 66-68, 93-95; *see also* Grasping, Head-shaking, Rooting
Mouth, *see* Feeding, Hand, Nursing
Mouth-grasping, 110
Movement
goal-specific, 15-17
perseveration of, 32
Musculature, maturation of, 53, 93, 107-112
Mythology, 87

Narcissism, 115, 120-122
Need gratification, 65-66, 89-93, 110, 126, 136-139, 145-149; *see also* Gratification, Hallucinatory gratification
Negation, xii, 71, 86-89, 99-102, 145-148, 150
acquisition of, by child, 56-57
as mental operation, 52-53, 100-102
Negative cephalogyric motion, 11-15, 34-40, 59, 70-71, 83
Negativism, 37, 100
Neonate, 19-22, 146
effect of filling stomach, 75-81
Neurology, 20
Nirvana principle, 38, 79, 90
"No"
acquisition of, 43-49, 56-59, 99-102, 129-131, 144-150
as abstraction, 99-102
as organizer of psychic development, 144-150
gesture, *see* Hand, Head-shaking "No"
motor prototype, *see* Rooting
verbal, 131-132, 139, 150
Nursing
and mimetic behavior, 67-68
behavior, 19-33, 67-69, 108-116
in preliterate societies, 97-98
termination of, by child, 93-95
see also Feeding

Nunberg, H., 118, 132, 157

Object
anaclitic choice of, 83
libidinal (love), 46-49, 56-59, 125-136, 144
need-gratifying, 57, 81, 128
see also Object relations, Self
Objectivation, 39, 53, 123, 127-130
Object relations
anaclitic, 57
and communication, 26, 36, 60, 69, 94, 149-150
and self-awareness, 120-123
and turning active, 45-48
and verbal expression of aggression, 131-136
earliest, ix, 5, 122-125
formation of, in infant with atresia esophagi, 71-85
inception of reciprocal, 94
matrix of, 80, 83-85
proper, 122, 125-131
role of imitation in, 41-42
see also Development, Identification, Mother
Oedipal phase, 46
Omnipotence, 121, 139-140
Ontogenesis, and phylogenesis, 24-26, 70, 81-83, 106, 147-148
Oral (Orality)
behavior, earliest, 68-69
by-passing of cathexis of zone, 70-85
orientation reflex, 21-22, 29, 62
phase, 83-85
triad, 75-81
see also Feeding, Nursing, Rooting
Organizers of psychic development, 83, 142-150
Orientation behavior, 20-22, 111-112
Ostow, M., 65, 157

Paramecium, 25, 92
Para-oral food intake, 84
Parents, imitation of child, 41-42, 98-99
Passivity, *see* Activity

[169]

INDEX

Tilney, F., 10, 27, 30-32, 35, 62-63, 75, 107, 159
Tinbergen, N., 22, 30, 159
"Transactions," 71
Transference, 61, 140
Traumatic neurosis, 110, 114
Trial-and-error behavior, 25, 92
Tropism, 145

Unconscious, 90, 104-105, 146
Undifferentiated phase, 38-40, 48, 87, 94, 96
Undoing, 114
Unpleasure
  and aggression, 47, 51, 56-58
  and cephalogyric motion, 10-11, 16, 67
  and dream screen, 76-80
  avoidance of, 76-77
  see also Frustration

Vision
  and dream screen, 77-79

and nursing, 110-114
in orientation of precocials, 29-30
  see also Perception
Vocalization of infants, 5-6, 63-64
Volition, 90, 94, 127, 136-141
von Senden, M., 159

Warren, H., 127, 159
Watson, J. B., 17, 159
Weaning, 123-125
Wolk, K., 110
Words
  global, 99-100
  primal, 95-96

"Yes"
  differentiation from "No," 96, 147
  motor prototype, 103-116
  see also Affirmation, Head-nodding

Zappert, J., 12, 159
Zeigarnik, B., 44, 159
Zubin, J., 159